CARE-FULL LOVE

Learning the joys and struggles of caregiving

BY

LOIS WERTH MIMBS

xulon PRESS

FOREWORD

by Jack Hayford

*T*he string of my fifty-seven years of pastoral ministry (and still counting) have two ends to it: the beginning years of preparation and the present years of confirmation and revelation moving toward life's finale in this world (*with another one waiting for each of us who will humbly make arrangements with and through the only One who can provide reservations*).

The beginning years immediately following high school were years of pursuit—of preparation via college and graduate work—studying at LIFE Bible College (Los Angeles) and Azusa Pacific College (Southern California). Filled with everything from college dorm life and campus good times to courtship and marriage (in my senior year), they all were overlaid with a serious quest to equip for a life as a pastor—a shepherd of souls. Packed with academic demand and spiritual growth, those years were marked by the constant flow of pragmatic wisdom and life-experience, understanding and instruction gained from gifted teachers and mentors—all experienced professors groomed through years in the parsonage, pulpit, and pressure cooker of the pastorate.

Not the least of the wonderful benefits accruing during those early years was the enriching and enjoyment found in friendships formed with other committed young men and women, individuals and couples who, like me, were dedicating their lives to the ministry of the gospel of Jesus Christ. Scores of solid relationships grew as together we prepared to shepherd God's flock as pastors and to labor in advancing the impact of local churches across our nation and to the nations of the world.

I was entering my junior year when I met Al Mimbs. He was so soft-spoken a guy that at first you could easily over-look that he was even in the room. However, he was also both an extremely gentlemanly and handsome guy, which ensured that if you didn't notice him, you did notice that any girls in the room did! Our acquaintance developed by reason that we both worked in downtown LA, had the same schedule for early afternoon jobs, and rode the same busses since we worked at office buildings less than two blocks apart. As a result, the many conversations we had en route to and from work provided the setting for our gaining a sense of one another's values and goals, and a friendship was shaped which continued into the years to come.

When Anna and I married, we regularly invited Al to dinner, and the common bond of our envisioned mission for our lives, along with the shared experiences of class and college life, did the rest to seal what became a lifelong friendship. About two years after Al took his first pastorate in Alabama, Anna and I were traveling through the South in national youth ministry. His pastorate in Sylacauga had been providentially scheduled for us, and our brief visit with Al was surprisingly enhanced when we discovered he had begun courting a beautiful young woman named Lois. (Impressed, we affirmed our approval—however, it was already becoming clear that Al didn't need it!)

While our friendship extended through all the years of Al's lifetime, our contact became sporadic. The region in which God's call placed each of our respective ministries put Anna and me half a nation apart from Al. Usually we would see each other only at our church's annual conference, and

I will always remember the delight we experienced the year
he arrived with Lois—his bride, who now partnered with
him in the pastoral ministry they served for scores of years.
Yet, while declaring we were "best" friends may seem gra-
tuitous to some, I always felt it was still true. Whenever we
saw each other at various church leadership conferences, we
instantly "picked up where we left off." The depth of our
regard for one another was obvious, and the sporadic lapses
of time together reduced nothing of the proposition: yes, we
were...*best friends!*

As time went by, we increasingly witnessed the richness
of Al and Lois' relationship. It was clear that the early obser-
vations about the treasure Al had found, and "what a perfect
couple they make," were precisely on target. God had given
Lois a truly good and gracious man, and He had given Al
a wife who was a woman of remarkable gifts—yet never
self-impressed and always unpretentious notwithstanding
her giftedness. Their love and commitment to each other,
as well as their joint call to ministry, was never in question:
Al and Lois were a couple whose life purpose was to serve
others and to do so skillfully—to serve with the liberality
that characterized our Savior, Jesus Christ, whom they represented with fidelity and integrity, true to God's Word, loving
those in need and unswerving in the clarity of their mission.

Their devotion to God was steadfast over the decades
of their ministering together amid the beauty of America's
Deep South until Al's health and mobility began to decline
due to an undiagnosed disease that eventually necessitated
his needing total care. That portion of their journey was not
a short one, becoming a distinct and trying time of ongoing
affliction. However, those years contain their own rich message of meaning and hope—meaning that will enrich you as
you read these pages.

It was during this time that Al and Lois faced the
dilemma inherent in those cases where medical advances

have extended life, yet illness and disease persist, mercilessly depriving one of health, mobility, and comfort. This scenario is compounded when death, though not exactly "at the door," is still inescapably couched nearby. The consequent dilemma is all too common: nursing home with round-the-clock "professional" care or full-time care-giving at home, with all its incumbent sacrifices?

That dilemma is exactly what onlookers witnessed as Al's debilitation progressed. For Lois, there was never a question. Friends and relatives looked on, their hearts filled with respect, as she took on the role of caregiver for her beloved husband. Lois' love for Al became all the more respected as we observed her steadfast constancy and unwavering fidelity to love's vows.

Anna and I were not able to be at Al's bedside as the time of his exit drew near, nor were we able to attend his memorial service. However, had I been there, I feel confident I would have been invited to express some personal sentiments to those family and friends gathered in Al's honor. There are two things I would have addressed.

First, Al Mimbs will always be remembered as being "pure gold." There is no higher assessment, because the value is essentially in the nature and quality found, not in the quantity of achievements or deeds. Life isn't measured by "how many" of anything we garner, gain, or grub to gather. Rather it is measured by the imprint we leave behind, the measure of our "presence" over time. This—and the truly abiding value of any individual—distills through how much of ourselves we give to others. It evolves from the ways we steward the life given us, how well we distribute the true stuff of life to those we live with, encounter, or work around. It manifests in how we purely, purposefully, and practically made their life richer because we remained on point, stood in the gap, and were there when and where it counted.

Al Mimbs was all this! He was, as we say, the real deal.

However, he would be the first to immediately push back these words of praise if he were here. If he accepted any such accolade, he would only do so as he pointed to his life-partner in marriage, saying, "That's more like her, not me." In truth, the description well applies to both Al and Lois.

If you knew Al, you can see his face, hear his voice, and imagine the gestures accompanying the words of denial I wrote above: "That's her, not me!" To even think of that makes me smile, but it leads me to the second thought I would have expressed had I been present for his memorial. Give me a moment to explain.

During our junior and senior years of college, Anna and I lived about a half-mile from the campus, and the shortest route there went right by a huge three-story house elevated on the side of a hill rising steeply above the street. It was where Al—still single—lived; his apartment perched in the highest corner of the great structure and gave a view toward LA's famous Echo Park Lake, which stretched for nearly a mile south of our campus.

My class schedule always differed from Al's, and most mornings I would pass by his house, his top-story window being always wide open for fresh air while he slept. I would often lift something of a "chant" from the street level as I passed. I knew he was likely still dozing in bed, with another twenty minutes probably available, but on some mornings my "college guy mood" got the better of me. When it did, I would call out like an ancient sea captain, *"Ahoy, matey!"* If I didn't get a response, I'd lift the call again as I continued walking down the street toward campus.

I could imagine Al's grin, along with his mild irritation at my stirring his slumber. As I continued on toward the campus, I would often hear a response, something like an echo floating above that LA neighborhood: *"Ahoy, matey!"* I always knew it was he, because there was something of the "Southern gentleman" in the soft, extended drawl of a now-grown Georgia boy that gave a Deep South flavor to his answering chant. I would laugh every time, not only because I had roused the sleeper, but because there was something about so simple an exchange that made me feel the strength of a bond between two young men who had met early on the pathway of following God's Son—both answering that call to do His will and to yield to His purpose for a lifetime.

Now Al's earthly mission is fully complete. And when Anna and I first received word of his homegoing, I must confess I sat down—touched to the core with a mix of grief and yet relief for both him and Lois. The ordeal was over, and Al was now "home at the Father's house." But while weeping, thinking, and praising God—a curious but proper mixture— suddenly a deep warmth swept over me and I broke into a smile that spread across my whole face.

I still smile with an inner joy when I remember it, because in that moment I imagined I could hear the call of my brother Al, wafting from somewhere in the world beyond this one, as he lifted a familiar chant to affirm his arrival—like a captain sailing into his harbor and home: *"Ahoy, matey! All is well—and I'm home to stay!"*

So now I welcome you to these pages. As you read, you'll discover some precious things about that last journey of his. Further, if you've never met Lois, you're going to be heart-warmed as you read of moments and anecdotes, experiences and wisdom found as she relates so many things that she and Al gained in the life journey they made together until death parted them.

Reading her narrative, you'll also discover that she is the crown jewel that God set into the "pure gold" that constituted Al Mimbs, and I have a prediction to propose: I think you may come to find them "best friends" as your take-away from this book.

The best part is this: you won't be able to resist recognizing something "extra," something of the timeless wealth and richness wrapped in the love of God—the living Lord they served all their life together. He is Jesus the Savior—the Lord of all and the one also often referred to as the Captain of our salvation.

He pilots a tight ship, but He invites all who will to come aboard.

"Ahoy, matey!"

Pastor Jack W. Hayford
Chancellor
The King's University-Los Angeles

ACKNOWLEDGMENTS

With deepest gratitude:

To my dear, sweet Al, who sacrificed time with me, watching quietly from his wheelchair as I sat for hours at the computer,

To my skilled editor, Angie Kiesling, for her talent in making the book flow,

To James Gilbert for totally taking over the electronic aspect of the book, patiently and expertly untangling my many messes,

To Pam Anderson, who was always on call when I ran into difficulty on my laptop,

To the multitude of friends and family, far and near, past and present, too numerous to list, who prayed for us and whose love for both Al and me constantly provided encouragement.

DEDICATION

*T*o Al, my sweetheart, my love, my darling husband of forty-five years, I thank you. I thank you for loving me unconditionally, for the lifetime of memories we shared, and for a love I will cherish forever.

TABLE OF CONTENTS

INTRODUCTION

BETWEEN THE ROCK AND A HARD PLACE

Who better to describe the path of experience than one who has walked it? Statistics show that 61.6 million people are now caregivers. With increased longevity, more and more people are facing the tough issue of needing someone to step up to the plate. Widespread cancer, diabetes, and heart disease—all having increased in recent years—require affordable care.

Out of my experiences of caring for my husband, Al, over the past eleven years, perhaps I can be an encouragement to someone else in similar circumstances. The apostle Paul writes in 2 Corinthians 1:3-5, "Blessed be the God and Father of our Lord Jesus Christ, the Father of mercies and God of all comfort, who consoles us in our every trouble, so that we may be able to encourage those in any kind of distress with the consolations with which we are divinely sustained. For as we experience richly the sufferings of Christ, so we enjoy through Christ an abundance of consolation."

Once in the middle of the night a short time into Al's undiagnosed illness, when I was particularly stressed and felt alone, I crept out of bed and tiptoed to the den where I thumped into the recliner and cried out to God, weeping copious tears and telling Him that I could not handle this whole thing. What was fast becoming evident was that I would be expected to take charge in a situation with which

I had absolutely no prior experience or training. I became overwhelmed with my role as caregiver, which came on much too fast and without a book of instructions.

After I poured out my grief and sadness, emotionally spent, I felt compelled to read Isaiah 46. Turning on the light to retrieve my Bible, I thought, *I know what chapter 43 says, I know what chapter 53 says, I know what chapter 61 says, I know . . .* , and I named all the scriptures I could remember from Isaiah, but chapter 46 did not ring a bell.

Opening the Word to Isaiah 46, I thought my impression must have been a mistake. But God does not make mistakes. At the fourth verse I read, "Even to old age I am the same and to the time of gray hair I will bear you ["bear" in Hebrew means "carry a heavy load"]. I have made you and I will carry you; even I will bear you and save you." How comforting!

I rejoiced and even saw some humor in the portion that says "to the time of gray hair" because I don't intend to ever have gray hair, so I'm covered forever! God knows exactly what we need and when.

How do these circumstances affect my life? A number of years ago, I attended a religious seminar at which the instructor asked us to develop a personal mission statement. That was no problem. I already knew: "To be conformed to the image of His Son . . ." (Romans 8:29). Then I began to question, is this illness of my beloved to "work together to conform me"? Is it to work through me, in me, with me? Is this situation, this trial, intended to fix *me*?

God in His wisdom knows what it will take to "fix" each of us. He knows what tools to use, for how long, and the amount of pressure He needs to apply. God deals with us on an individual basis. We're not cookie-cutter children who belong to God. Each of us is different.

That said, it's the same thing with the treatment designed to "help" our loved one. Al was not a cookie-cutter person;

he was not the same as the patient in the next room of the hospital, he was different from the other patients on the doctor's list for Wednesday afternoon, and he might have reacted differently to the same medication the doctor prescribed for John Doe yesterday. A caregiver must be alert for changes and problems that arise as a result of the person's individuality. We must be tenacious when those times come—and they will.

In each situation regarding Al's care, I knew I must take charge. I was his only advocate. I was totally responsible for making decisions he was no longer capable of making. At the onset of his illness, he was somewhat able to participate in conversations and understood to a great extent what was going on. However, he couldn't initiate thoughts and ideas, only respond—sometimes correctly, sometimes incorrectly. Asking his opinion, inquiring as to his input, and guiding him toward making decisions was very important. It helped him to feel that he was still an integral part in the scheme of things, and he seemed to shine when given the opportunity.

As time went on, this ability diminished. I learned, however, that it was still helpful and reassuring to him to be included whether or not his response was valid. In medical decisions, I remained assertive in order to prevent incorrect or unwise decisions by the medical community that would not be in his best interest. I had to become "Mama Bear," protecting her cubs. Other times I had to ride a broom. Keeping the balance between "nice" and "firm," and, yes, even "mean," was sometimes divided by a very fine line.

For example, at one time Al's primary care doctor suggested putting in a Foley catheter (though admittedly unnecessary) in order to qualify Al for Home Health visits–supposedly to help *me*. Perhaps his heart was in the right place when he made the suggestion. I listened to the doctor's explanation, but in the back of my mind I was thinking about how a catheter can cause urinary tract infections and other complications. Even if I could have computed in my brain that the decision would help me, I couldn't justify subjecting Al to further pain and discomfort. It was not a difficult decision. My immediate response was, "Not in this lifetime you won't!"

When I reflect on this incident I think, *What if I had not been there? Would they have followed through with their recommendation? Lord, help me to know when and how to make the correct decisions. Thank You for guiding me. And most of all help me to forgive those who I feel trespass against me and against Al. Help me to give them the benefit of the doubt.*

If you choose to care for your loved one at home, whether out of necessity or by choice, you will be tested with many challenges. You will feel that no one in the medical profession understands anything you sense and believe to be the right thing to do for your individual situation. Because you are together 24/7, you may ask, "Is anyone listening? How can they know this patient better than I?" They can't! And you would be right!

As you encounter some of the challenges surrounding the care of your loved one, the constant dealings with the healthcare community, the medical community, and the companies and personnel who control the strings holding certain equipment you need, you will feel that you are totally alone and that no one understands you. But let me assure you, I've been there and I do understand. Furthermore, if I can make it so can you.

In reflection, I have learned that I didn't always make the right decisions, whether out of ignorance or stubbornness, not understanding all the facts, or trying to favor Al and his circumstances. But, based on the knowledge and experience I had at the time, I endeavored to do what I felt was best for him.

This accounting shows that God is there with you. And

He will never leave you or forsake you. It is my privilege as Al's lifetime sweetheart to honor my wedding vows to love and care for him "in sickness and in health."

CHAPTER ONE

I SHALL NOT LIVE BY
BLUE EYES ALONE

*P*acking the car with only my clothes, I drove all night and finally arrived in a town about twenty miles from the school where I was going to teach. As a child, I'd always enjoyed playing school and pretending to be the teacher, so when an opportunity opened in Alabama for a teaching position at the School for the Deaf, I left my job at a stock brokerage in St. Louis and made plans to move down South. *Am I dreaming? Can I possibly know what I am doing?*

Slowly cruising the quiet streets, I noticed a nice two-story tourist home. Upon investigation, I learned it had an available room and private bath at a weekly rate. When I went to take a look at the room, a young man resident was sitting in a rocking chair on the porch reading the afternoon newspaper. As I approached the house, he slightly lowered his paper to see who was walking up. Wow! I was struck by the most beautiful crystal blue eyes I had ever seen making a quick assessment of my presence. Then he raised the paper to its former position and went back to reading.

I thought, *Who is connected to those gorgeous eyes?* Later I learned that those eyes belonged to a single pastor in town who had prayed that God would send him a wife to share in the ministry. He decided, however, in the five seconds of peering across the top of the paper that, "Nope, Lord, she's not the one."

I rented the first room down the hall; he lived in the second room. Over the next three or four months, I discovered Blue Eyes' name was Al. Yes, we lived in the same house. That is as far as it went.

One day several of the townspeople told Al they were planning to visit his church that next Sunday night. It turned out the owners of the tourist home and I attended the same church; I suppose they told him I could play the piano. He realized he had no one to play for the service so, panic-stricken, he invited me (through the bathroom wall) to please come to his church and provide music for that night. I agreed, and you would think that out of undying gratitude he would have taken me to dinner or something, but no. No such thing happened. Our relationship stayed platonic.

Almost a year later as we sat in the rocking chairs on the front porch just chatting, he said he had to fulfill his responsibility to attend his church's summer youth camp and needed to go inside and iron his shirts. I volunteered and meticulously steamed, buttoned, folded, and presented him with six expertly done sport shirts. Surely *now* he would take me to dinner, but no.

That summer, the woman who owned the tourist home became ill and needed my room, which necessitated my moving elsewhere in town. I found an apartment about six blocks away owned by a widow advertising to rent it. As it turned out, I rented a room in her home instead.

A year later, I was still teaching and during spring break went back to Illinois to visit my parents. The day I planned to return home my father died very unexpectedly of a heart attack. Thank God for His mercy that I was there. I don't think I could have survived a phone call bearing such horrible news. Al didn't attend the funeral but wired a dozen red roses. I was impressed with the fact that he showed compassion. But he remained very reserved.

Occasionally, well, more than occasionally, I found myself surreptitiously watching for his car to go by the house where I lived. I noticed that I began to wonder what he was doing, if he might be at the favorite restaurant in town. Maybe I could just happen to go there to eat and accidentally run into him. Would I admit that? Probably not. He didn't really give me the time of day. My hidden yearnings needed to stay that way, hidden, because apparently it was one-sided. Al also had to move from the tourist home and took up residence two blocks down the street from where I now lived. We dated occasionally, but it was usually just a "coke" date; he couldn't afford more than that. Another year passed and I decided to go to college in Florida for a year to major in music. I guess I was secretly hoping that "absence makes the heart grow fonder."

Maybe it worked a little, because one day when I opened mailbox number 7 there was an envelope with his handwriting. A letter! Wow! Again, very generic, non-commital. Overjoyed, I responded, but I was careful not to "throw myself at him." Was God actually working in his emotions?

During the school year, I went on a choir tour with the college. One scheduled performance was within driving distance for Al so he attended the concert. I was so looking forward to seeing him again. I made sure he could observe me as I laughed and teased with the guys in the choir. Strategy? Maybe. Afterwards, he offered to take me to the place I was staying, and for the first time he told me he loved me. Shocked and overwhelmed, I said, "Thank you." I can't help but chuckle each time I think of how romantic I was!

At the end of that school year, I moved back to the same residence where I had lived before. Al and I began to date exclusively and our relationship deepened, but another year passed before he proposed marriage. Five months later, on a beautiful September afternoon, the four o'clock wedding took place.

As I started down the aisle on my brother's arm, a large lump formed in my throat as thoughts about my father surfaced. *Oh, how I wish Daddy could be here to take his place beside me!* Copious tears flowed unchecked to the strains of "Trumpets Voluntary." They dripped into my veil and splashed onto the kneeling bench. The minister gave me his handkerchief during the ceremony. I cried all the more.

Worrying that I couldn't gain control of my emotions in order to sing to Al was uppermost in my mind. The song I had written was adapted from the words in Deuteronomy 6:24-25, "Let us commit our ways unto the Lord, our God, and love Him, and fear Him and keep his statutes as He has commanded us, for our good always, that He might preserve us alive as it is even at this day."

So it was with great difficulty I finally completed the song and the vows. When he lifted the veil to kiss me, several guests told me later that the sequins on my veil glistened beautifully in the candlelight. "Tears," I said, "not sequins."

Just who was this wonderful man I married? I'm so glad you asked!

CHAPTER TWO

MEET AL

*A*nother boy! Al was number seven of eight children born to his parents and reared in the Deep South, namely Macon, Georgia. Their mother, a godly woman, at times had to work outside the home because Mr. Mimbs became ill and then was seriously injured at work and unable to fully support the large family. Area churches that saw the family's need often came to the rescue with baskets of food and clothing, and at Christmastime they even provided gifts for the children.

As a young child, Al was extremely shy, hiding behind Mama's skirt whenever company came. At this point one would hardly have guessed he would become a public speaker someday, much less a minister. But God was at work in his life as Psalm 139:13-14 states, "You did possess my inward parts and did weave me in my mother's womb. I praise Thee because I have been fearfully and wonderfully made . . . Marvelous is Thy workmanship as my soul is well aware." And in verse 5, "Thou hast closed me in behind and in front, and has placed Thy hand upon me."

During Al's teen years, he attended Christian summer camps, all the time knowing in his heart he would one day be in full-time ministry, the result of a vision when God called him at the age of nine years. Following his high school graduation, he left home to travel across the United States to California to attend LIFE, a four-year Bible college. He finished with top honors.

Wanting to pastor in the Southeast where he would be familiar with the culture, Al learned from his district supervisor about a little church in a small town in Alabama. He described it as a pretty nice building with about thirty people, though not much salary. That was no problem for Al—in those early years he knew he would have to be bi-vocational.

Eager to try his wings, and with stars in his eyes, he agreed to take the position and drove from Los Angeles to Alabama in an old blue Buick he had bought from his older brother. Even though the car looked fairly good on the outside, the Naugahyde on the passenger's seat was split and handfuls of the stuffing had come out leaving a serious chasm. But, hey, it was a car!

Arriving in the small mill town, Al drove around the tree-lined streets until he came across a tourist home. Like other similar tourist homes it was a large two-story house with columns and a front porch that stretched the entire width of the house. Each furnished room had a private bath. It seemed to be within his meager budget, so he paid the first week's rent and moved in his few belongings. No food or kitchen privileges were available, but he discovered another bed-and-breakfast-type place a few blocks down the street that served home-style suppers five nights a week. He signed up and joined a number of the town's other professional people who had standing reservations there.

Now on to the task at hand. Al located the "pretty nice building" his district supervisor had told him about—with weeds more than knee-high, certainly no people to be found, and the pews piled up haphazardly in one corner of the sanctuary. The clerk at the drugstore next door, who he later learned was a very famous singer/actor's aunt, said the church had been closed for some time.

"Lord, have You brought me out here to starve? To become a laughingstock?" Al prayed. "Where shall I begin? Did I misread the directions? Should I have 'spied out the land' first?"

Before his enthusiasm waned, he waded into the high weeds with a mower and cut the grass, cleaned the inside of the dilapidated building, unstacked the pews, pronounced that the piano worked all right, and within about three weeks was open for business.

Studying late into the night and seeking God for direction, he fervently prepared to deliver his first sermon. Not a college assignment, not a practice, but a real launching of his life's career. Al was up long before daylight, showered and dressed in his finest for making his debut. A beautiful sunrise greeted him.

Arriving at the church very early to put the final touches on his sermon—and to be there when the crowd came—he wondered what lay ahead for him. "Lord, I surrender my life anew. Place Your Holy Spirit within me and fulfill Your purpose today as I serve in Your vineyard. May needy people come to know You and receive eternal life. Amen."

Rising from his knees, he paced, waiting with a hopeful heart. One, two, three, four curious people came one by one to see the new preacher in town.

He preached his heart out to a handful of people and thus began his pulpit ministry. Over the next few months, several young people came to faith in Christ. The immediate results he hoped for didn't happen, but Al was faithful to his flock. He taught them, prayed with them, led them, cared for them, and worked side by side, loving them through their spiritual struggles.

He immediately applied at the local high school for a substitute teaching position in math and English. Students were drawn to him because he identified with them and taught them accordingly. Even the teachers, upon returning to the classroom following their absence, complimented him on "getting through" to the students and asked how he did it. They admitted having tried unsuccessfully to teach a certain concept for weeks, and the students just didn't comprehend, then Al would accomplish it in a day or two.

The church building needed a lot of repair. One week a Sunday school teacher stepped out from the Christian education section and her foot and leg fell through the termite-ridden floor, rendering her helpless and creating a humorous sight. It was apparent the time had come to tear down the present building and move the small congregation into a nearby rental place on Sundays while the church was being rebuilt. Al and one of his high school students worked every day all summer to tear down the old building brick by brick with only a crowbar and a sledgehammer.

Then he hired a part-time brick mason who rebuilt the walls while Al mixed the cement and carried it up the ladder by bucketfuls to supply him with "mud." Many struggles ensued. The brick mason, when he did show up, would work only a couple of hours and then had to leave to visit his mistress. Unending fundraisers by the few faithful ladies of the congregation—candy sales, turkey dinners to deliver, homemade cakes to sell, yard sales—interspersed with many miracles, slowly but surely turned the dream into a reality.

Meanwhile, I showed up in the middle of all this, an answer to his prayer, I might say, even though he did not acknowledge me as such for several years! He finally "got the memo" and five years later we were married.

One of the miracles involved installing the church's electrical wiring. Someone in town suggested Al contact the nearby trade school, as paying an electrician to do the work was cost-prohibitive. He was teaching school, so I was appointed to call the notoriously cantankerous supervisor of the trade school to ask if he could help us. After making an appointment with me to tour the unfinished building, he agreed to take it on as a project for one of the classes studying to be electricians. I must say, he did not live up to the reputation circulating about him. He was an absolute gentleman and completely accommodating, cheerfully doing all the labor and supplying all the materials without charge.

As a single good-looking minister, Al had a lot of influence on the youth of the congregation. A number of them were from "the projects" in this little mill town, but he recognized immediately that they were very intelligent and determined to rise above their difficulties and make something of themselves. Al encouraged them in every aspect of their lives. As they grew up, a high ratio of the teenagers went to college and majored in subjects that afforded them top-paying jobs.

Al identified with one little guy who had a speech impediment, and even though Al was not trained in speech therapy, he spent hours helping the young man develop skills to improve his speech. Now grown up, married, the father of several children, and even a grandfather, he recently sent us pictures of the house he built for his family. His sister became a registered nurse and has just retired. Their brother is the CEO of a large company. Their ninety-one-year-old mother who attended Al's first church service declares that "Brother Mimbs" deserves a lot of credit for their success.

Another young lady learned to play the piano from Al, who had with God's help taught himself to play. As an adult she has served as pianist/organist at her church for years. One of the other girls has a degree in math, has authored several books on aviation, and flies her own plane. Her sister is an author and playwright and is being published now. She is a licensed clinical psychotherapist who specialized in working with traumatized children. They were all in elementary school when Al came to their town.

When this miracle church was finally completed, we enjoyed our first service and dedication of the new building.

The entire congregation from a neighboring church of a different denomination who had helped us with numerous fundraisers joined us for that service to show their support. What a day of celebration it was! The following Sunday, Al resigned as their pastor, and the next Sunday was our final Sunday. Al had completed fourteen years of work, struggle, learning, and faithfulness. It was time to move on.

Al had pastored single for eight years. Following our wedding, he started teaching at the Alabama State School for Deaf where I taught for five years. The night before he started teaching fourth grade math to the children, I taught him the alphabet and the signs for add, subtract, multiply, and divide. The students loved helping him learn what they knew so well.

We worked there together for two years, still pastoring, and then branched out to public school. Al was a guidance counselor at a county middle school and I taught first grade for one year, then received a full college scholarship. After six years of teaching, pastoring, and working together to complete the church building we accepted a new appointment in Georgia.

His influence continued in the next church. For example, a teenage couple came to faith in Christ, and after working in the church with us for a couple of years, they left the area to attend Bible college to prepare for ministry. The first in their families to go to college, they both went on to secular colleges for their degrees. Over his lifetime in Christian service, the husband served as a pastor, overseer of a church television ministry, and vice president of a large corporation. His wife has a master's degree and teaches. Their children are college educated and the story continues. They have enjoyed material blessings, but the most important thing is that they have continued to serve God and follow Him.

Through Al's encouragement, they in turn have influenced many members of their families who accepted Christ and have also gone on to college and to serve the Lord. They readily accepted his advice because they saw his example. He did not become wealthy, but he showed them that getting an education would provide many more opportunities to excel in life. Learning to put God first was his ultimate challenge to them.

Three more congregations in Al's ministry produced youth leaders who went on to pastor their own churches, and couples who served under Al are missionaries with extensive ministries throughout the world. Two couples have started numerous Bible schools around the globe, spreading the gospel to areas where we could not go. But we have continued to support them both financially and with prayer. How pleased we are to know that the Great Commission goes on!

Al received his fifty-year service award in October 2007 from the denomination he served even though he could no longer be active. I remember his telling me early on that we did not need to save for retirement because he would die preaching. That was his heart's desire. Though his dream was shattered by illness, nevertheless we thank God that He is faithful!

I remembered back to when we repeated our vows, including "in sickness and in health." At the time we had no idea what lay ahead for us. The beautiful autumn day filled with joy, friends' congratulatory wishes, and our expectations of a life of promise revealed not one hint of the struggles and sorrow that would eventually consume our lives.

Originally, I planned to describe these experiences and feelings without reference to the most important aspect of my life, my faith and trust in God. I reasoned that other caregivers who don't choose to embrace my love for and dependence on God would feel "that is all right for you, and maybe your God helps you, but I don't believe that way and it's just a crutch." I realized they in turn may discount the portion that has sustained me many, many times. But I must include my greatest source of strength.

Throughout my entire life, I have depended on God to be my constant companion, to guide me, and to be my healer and provider. Needless to say, each situation has been laced with prayer.

CHAPTER THREE

SOMETHING IS WRONG!

"*A*l, what is wrong? Are you sick? Talk to me!" I could hardly distinguish his words.

While I was in Illinois in 1996 visiting my mother in a nursing home, Al phoned me. I knew immediately something was terribly wrong. My normally vibrant sixty-one-year-old husband didn't sound like himself. He was very weak, but he was able to tell me he was acutely ill with what he guessed to be a virus. His stomach had always been very sensitive, even to a change in drinking water. I knew he must be fearful because he had a history of going into shock and fainting when he vomited. From experience, it was obvious that he needed me.

I was torn between my mother's need for my attention and Al's need of my help at home. I checked in almost hourly on his condition. He was suffering very high fevers, diarrhea, vomiting, weakness, and dizziness; he was almost unable to get out of bed. What should I do? I had driven almost five hundred miles to be with Mother. But Al's being so very ill and alone concerned me deeply.

I decided to cut my visit short and go home. By the time I arrived, Al had improved a little but was very weak. During his recovery from the virus, he battled fatigue, occasional loss of memory, some confusion, and had difficulty keeping his balance. After consulting our general practitioner, he prescribed physical therapy by Home Health. But attempts to correct his coordination failed; he couldn't seem to transfer the information from his brain to his muscles.

Al's acute symptoms lessened somewhat, but the effects lingered for months. It seemed that from then on he was never the same. It wasn't something that could be pinpointed or described, just different.

Going to the doctor was frustrating. Our family doctor said it was a virus that was going around. He didn't know what to do or how to treat Al, and what, if any, medication would help. Symptoms were masked or else masqueraded as something else.

After several weeks of slowly recovering, he insisted he could drive. Two blocks to the post office, one block to the church, three blocks to the bank. He assured me, "As long as I am sitting down, I'm all right."

"What will happen when you reach your destination? You can't just sit in the car!" I held my breath each time he left the house.

Prior to this virus episode, he had enjoyed meeting church friends at the walking track. Once he lost his balance and actually fell, skinning his face and hands on the pavement.

At home, he played in the yard with our Pek-a-Poo. It often resulted in his falling in the grass and having to crawl to the porch and use the banister to pull himself upright. Coming down the hallway from the bedroom, Al would go from side to side, bouncing from one wall to the other as he attempted to walk to the living room.

Lord, what is wrong? What has happened to my dear sweetheart? What can I do?

Watching Al go from a gifted, talented, competent individual who was completely self-sufficient and agile to becoming an unbalanced, forgetful person struggling to walk was heartbreaking. He had difficulty just staying awake during his study time. Each doctor visit was more frustrating than the last. No one knew what to do.

Unprecedented episodes began to take place. One Sunday morning while he was showering, he lost his balance and fell, bringing down the shower rod and curtain. Loud clattering followed by a thud sent me running to the bathroom. I found Al lying across the bathroom floor, his feet still in the shower stall. Water was spraying everywhere!

Stepping over his body, I reached to turn off the water. Through our tears of sadness at the realization of yet another incident of helplessness, he and I struggled together to get him into an upright position. We needed to finish rinsing the soap out of his hair and off his body. I had already dressed for church, so by this time I had to start over. More tears.

When the nightmare of intermittent periods of incontinence began to occur, we were devastated. If I reminded him that he would not want the problem to happen in public, he remained in denial and didn't want to accept my help. As he dressed for church one Sunday, I tactfully suggested maybe he could put a pad into his underwear to prevent an accident in public. He said there was nothing wrong with him and he didn't need my help. My heart was breaking!

Lord, please show him that I'm only trying to help. I want to protect him from embarrassment, to do what I can until we find out what is wrong.

While I was dealing with what could be done to fix this, several of the young fellows at church were helping him to his chair on the platform before the Sunday morning service. Looking down at his feet, they asked where the "water" on the carpet was coming from.

Waiting nearby with the choir to go out, I quickly covered the situation by saying, "Oh, I spilled that earlier when I was watering the plants at the front of the sanctuary." They just accepted the explanation and moved on. I was thankful they didn't press the issue, but at the same time I was dying inside. Could we find something good in this situation? Yes, thank the Lord, he was wearing a dark suit!

Leaving him alone was of great concern to me. I was fearful of how I might find him when I returned. Would he be safe while I was gone? Would he hurt himself or fall?

We must *do* something! But I drew a blank when it came to deciding on a starting place. So far the medical community had not been able to offer a solution.

This problem had to have something to do with a malfunction in the brain, so we took a stab in the dark and made an appointment with a neurologist. "Time's a'wastin'," as Snuffy Smith used to say in the comic strip. Even yesterday wouldn't be soon enough. I felt as if we were walking in quicksand. Would the appointment day ever arrive? Struggling through each day experiencing new and various changes, the days seemed weeks long. Finally the day actually came.

We were ushered into a well-appointed office where a handsomely dressed young man sat. He sported Italian leather shoes, a monogrammed shirt, and wore a pleasant smile. As we talked and answered each other's questions, we didn't seem to connect. The atmosphere felt a bit tense. But since it was our first experience, we didn't really know what to expect. We finally said our goodbyes and confirmed our appointment for two weeks later.

After leaving the appointment, I began to picture how busy the neurologist would be, researching, consulting his reference books, scheduling tests, discussing with colleagues this new patient whose symptoms were outside the box, not fitting any ordinary profile of most known diseases. My anticipations and expectations matched my level of excitement at what we would learn at the next appointment. Soon this mystery would be solved. Soon we would know what could be done to help Al get better.

We felt like children waiting for Christmas; it seemed like forever. Eventually, however, the time gap closed and we again entered the same lovely office and were greeted by the same impeccably-dressed neurologist. After seating himself, he leaned back in his chair, clasped his hands behind his head, smiled at us, and asked, "So why are you here today?"

Instantly, my brain exploded and my entire being flooded with anger and disbelief. I came up out of my chair, my voice on edge. All the pent-up emotions of the preceding weeks spewed out. Al tried to pull me down and calm me. I was not to be calmed. I screeched, "What? What have you been doing for the last two weeks?"

He acted as if he had never seen us before. We were just another client keeping any other appointment. My disappointment could not be measured. Hot tears welled up in my eyes and spilled down my cheeks. My breath came in short gasps. Why didn't he have any answers? Why had he not become involved in our frustration and devastation? Did he not realize how important it was for us to have some kind of help? Al had a profession and could not go stumbling around not knowing what was happening to him. Couldn't he see how we were grasping at straws?

Lord, if this is Your idea of conforming me to the image of Your Son, You can forget it! This is not funny. I cannot take this!

I tried to calm down but my brain was still clouded with anger. After sitting stone-faced in silence to gain my composure, I attempted to ask civil questions. The doctor stated that he was referring us to someone at Vanderbilt in Nashville. I let his statement sink in and reasoned, *Well, at least maybe we can talk to someone who* will *be able to help us.*

Dejected, I walked out of the office, totally numb.

Turmoil reigned in my spirit. Questions remained unanswered. *Lord, can I risk hoping again? With Your help, can we bounce back?* Emotional recovery was like a rollercoaster.

But given time, repentance, and prayer, hope was slowly renewed as we awaited the time for the visit with the "specialist." Al continued to sleep a lot, have poor balance, and need more and more assistance.

In preparation for the appointment, I had to make long-distance calls numerous times to ensure that all medical records were not only sent but also had been received by the specialist.

When the day arrived, we excitedly made the three-hour trip to Nashville where we were shown into the new doctor's office. A relaxed, casually-dressed man entered the room, shook hands with us, smiled pleasantly, and seated himself. He picked up a stack of folders and read the names until he got to ours. When he opened the folder, I observed that the folder was empty except for the intake information containing our name, address, and phone number.

Round TWO! I raised my voice, asking in total disbelief, "Where are the records I requested be sent to you?"

He put his index finger to his lips and whispered, "Shhh, it's okay; we have fax machines. It will be only a matter of minutes and we will retrieve them."

"But I worked so hard to get them for you in advance so you could be familiar with Al's case before we arrived," I protested.

"Shhh," he whispered again. "It's okay." Then he stepped out of the room to ask his assistant to get the records. My thoughts roiled within me. *This is our money you're spending! Doesn't anybody care?*

I was furious, frustrated, confused, and disappointed once again, disgusted at the incompetence and lack of professionalism. What had become of all my efforts to have everything in place for a smooth and profitable meeting? Why didn't someone besides me see how important this issue was?

When he returned, he still had no records but started the session with various questions. Having worked in the mental health field in an administrative capacity, I recognized that our so-called specialist was a psychiatrist! And soon I further learned that our appointment was designed, not for Al, but for me. I was the crazy woman; poor Al was the victim!

He continued the session by asking Al what profession he was in, which he would have learned from the records if he had received them. Al replied, "I am a minister, a pastor."

The doctor's eyes got very large, his eyebrows went up in surprise, and he turned to me and said in disbelief, *"And you're a pastor's wife!"*

"Yes," I said, squaring my shoulders, "and I'm a darn good one."

We were subsequently dismissed from his office, and once again I was in a daze. The three-hour trip home was quiet. Probably each of us was thinking the same thing, but it was too painful to express those thoughts.

What was accomplished in this interview? All right, so Al couldn't remember to repeat ten minutes later the doctor's three unrelated words in a row. I knew that before we went because many "normal" people can't do it either. Had we wasted our time and money? Can you imagine my reaction when the secretary called us for information in order to send us a bill? I considered saying, "I thought you had fax machines." Instead I said, "In your dreams!"

She responded, "I certainly understand," and hung up the phone.

Heartbreak...frustration...puzzlement...confusion. *What can we do? It must be something neurological. Can anything be done to fix this? Is there any hope? What are we missing? Where can we go now?*

CHAPTER FOUR

TESTING, TESTING, 1, 2, 3

*M*ayo Clinic! Not Mayo Clinic! That place is reserved as a last resort for the critically, incurably ill. What could we learn there? By this time Al had been deteriorating gradually for about two years, and no one was coming up with a reason or a diagnosis. So Al's new neurologist determined that he needed to go to Rochester, Minnesota, for further testing.

Upon arriving at the hotel, we discovered it was actually connected by underground passageways to the clinic. In other words, we never had to go outside unless we chose. We were prepared to stay four days to meet their schedule of appointments, so we thought we had everything covered. But God knew our future and took care of us. Four days suddenly turned into ten days. Thank God, He is our Jehovah Jireh, our Provider.

The Sunday before we left home, two individuals in our church family suggested that the congregation take an offering to help fund our trip. What a loving gesture!

At the clinic, diagnostic attempts included tests for multiple sclerosis, muscular dystrophy, Lyme's disease, Lou Gehrig's disease, and any and all other muscle diseases. Blood tests, scans, X-rays, and biopsies were conducted. If there was a test, we had it.

However, after all the testing and expense of ten days at the famous Mayo Clinic, they did not have a diagnosis. Al's body was seemingly healthy. His blood pressure was perfect at 120/70, and he had no heart disease, diabetes, or any other maladies. He took no medication. But the MRI of his brain showed white areas indicating that the brain was shrinking. The nearest diagnosis was cerebellar atrophy, but it did not fit the profile either. One of the reports stated that he had ataxia, an inability to coordinate voluntary muscle movements, symptomatic of some nervous disorders. This was certainly no new revelation. We already knew that.

Six months prior to our Mayo Clinic visit, Al's one-year-older brother who lived in Texas had been having a balance problem also. He experienced a motor vehicle accident requiring him to be hospitalized briefly. An MRI was done to check for brain injury. Impatient and insisting he was all right, he checked himself out of the hospital. His doctor strongly advised against his decision because he lived alone. About a week later, he was found dead in his home from complications of diabetes.

We requested that a copy of his MRI be sent to Al's neurologist, who discovered that Al's X-rays and his brother's X-rays were interchangeable. It was shocking! Apparently, his brother's disease had not progressed as far as Al's because he was still driving.

While we were at the clinic I kept a record of all our expenditures, large and small, and we had sufficient funds with literally about twelve dollars to spare. What would we have done without the additional funds? Matthew 6:26 says, "Look at the birds of the air, how they neither sow nor reap nor gather into barns, but your heavenly Father feeds them. Are not you more valuable than they?" (New Berkeley Version)

CHAPTER FIVE

LET'S PLAY MARBLES

*P*rojectile vomiting—not a very pleasant thing, but also not completely unusual for Al. In my general reading I came across an account of another person who had ongoing projectile vomiting caused by problems in the cerebellum, the part of the brain that is said to control vomiting. Was this also a possibility in Al's case? He too had been given an "iffy" diagnosis of cerebellar atrophy, even though most of the symptoms did not fit the profile. Then almost overnight his urine changed to the color of coffee, and high fevers with a rapid heart rate accompanied the vomiting.

Al was admitted to the hospital where a CAT scan was done. It was discovered that he had about ten marble-sized stones in the common bile duct. Since it was a small hospital, they did not have a surgeon on staff so he was transferred to a larger hospital for surgery.

We were very comfortable going to the larger hospital because Al had seen a gastroenterologist there, had a cholesysectomy there, and the surroundings and staff were familiar to us. After Al was admitted, another X-ray was taken. At my request to see the X-ray, the doctor obliged. I was astonished at the "stack" of stones, side by side, some perfectly round, some slightly lopsided and packed against each other, but it definitely showed a full duct of stones. Could this be the cause of a great deal of his pain?

Surgery was scheduled for the next day. He was wheeled into the holding room. I kissed Al and told him I'd see him in a little while. Within about twenty minutes, the urologist doing the surgery came to the waiting room and explained that he was unable to remove the stones. Scar tissue had developed as a result of previous surgeries, and Al's anatomy was sort of "upside down." In other words, his insides had shifted. The doctor's instrumentation was not adequate to complete the surgery.

Questions tumbled through my brain. *What does this mean? Where do we go from here? Is Al going to be all right? What are our options? Can this be fixed?*

"We have three options," the doctor explained. "One, we can send him to Vanderbilt where they may be able to get them out. Two, we can open him up and remove them surgically, and we would have to engage a surgeon to do this, or three, we can just leave them in there."

My mind raced. *This decision is in my hands at this moment. What will be the consequences of each of the decisions? I need Your help, Lord.*

"Doctor," I said, "if he were your brother, what would you do?" The question hung in the air. Suddenly, the decision had a different slant. Silence ensued. The doctor finally recovered enough to process my question.

"Okay," he began, "I think I would have the surgery and have the stones removed." That was my inclination also, but I needed reassurance. That settled it.

Then he dropped a bomb. "I'll go ahead and schedule Dr. So-and-So to do the surgery. . ."

My insides lurched, and panic gripped my heart. I threw up my hands and covered my face, and without even thinking I blurted "NO!" He was understandably stunned. I apologized for my reaction and begged him not to require an explanation.

What flashed into my mind were experiences in our role as pastors. We knew of three different parishioners who had Dr. So-and-So do surgery on them, and with each one their routine situations became nearly fatal.

There was no way I could put Al's life into the hands of a person with that reputation in surgery. I did not want to divulge this information to another doctor. Thinking back, maybe I should have. Was it just coincidence? Was it incompetence? My mind continued to whirl.

I inquired about the surgeon who had done Al's gall bladder surgery. He was out of town until Monday. I asked if we could wait. He said we could, but Al would have to stay at the hospital over the weekend. It was too risky in case he encountered an emergency. I agreed, and it was settled.

No one at the hospital ever knew why my reaction was so adamant, but I knew I had made the right decision. On Monday, our trusted doctor prepared to do the surgery and graciously allowed me to be with Al right up to the moment they called him into the holding room. The doctor's prayer with us was such a comfort.

He did the surgery and was able to go in at the site of a previous scar from when Al had a gastrectomy twenty years before. Scar tissue had caused his stomach not to empty properly, so 48 percent of his stomach as well as the duodenum had to be removed.

After the stones were removed, Al was placed in a room and as usual the nursing staff came and went, checking on him and giving the prescribed medication. He had a fairly peaceful night. I remained at his bedside. The next day they started a soft diet, which he promptly hurled. The product he regurgitated resembled coffee grounds. The doctor was notified and without my knowledge a nurse gave him an injection of 25 mg of Phenergan along with Demerol to help him relax and to stop the vomiting. When I inquired what the medication was, the nurse skirted the issue. With persistence, I was able to extract the information from her.

I explained that he was very sensitive to medication. If Phenergan was ever given, he could tolerate only 12.5 mg, only half of what they were giving him. Three hours later he vomited again, and in she came with more of the same medications. I asked her to please not give him any more, but she claimed doctor's orders and gave him another 25 mg of Phenergan plus Demerol for pain.

Within minutes, I couldn't get Al to respond to me. He wouldn't open his eyes or give any indication that he could hear me. I checked his pulse. It was very slow and weak. Respiration was shallow. I turned on the call light to summon a nurse; she asked what I needed. I told her, and she said okay, but no one ever came. I stepped into the hall to see if I could get someone's attention. Panic began to overtake me. I begged a different nurse who happened to be passing the room to please check on Al. I explained that I couldn't get him to respond.

She assessed the situation and called the emergency response team of five people who came almost immediately. After a brief evaluation, they determined that he was overdosed and quickly moved him to ICU. The doctor was notified and they started procedures to detoxify his system. His temperature soared while he lay motionless, barely breathing. They worked for hours wiping him down with cool wet cloths to reduce the fever. Electric fans were positioned to cool his almost bare body.

He continued to vomit so an NG tube was used to suction the contents of his stomach. After four days in ICU, he was finally moved to a room.

I preceded Al to the room. Lots of nurses accompanied his relocation, hooking up all the machines and tubes, doing intake procedures, asking questions, and completing records. Shortly after they all left, I realized that he was going to vomit, even though he had an NG tube. I quickly called the nurse. I told her Al was very nauseated and I suspected there may be something wrong with the NG tube.

"No, it can't be that; it's new and I just put it in," she answered sharply.

I said again, "Please, just check it." *Please listen to me; I know this patient very well. You just met him!* She was frustrated with my insistence, but she checked it and finally conceded sheepishly that the suction wasn't working. During this encounter, Al vomited. She went and got another unit and hooked it up. Al immediately settled down as the new unit started working properly. Chopped liver again? Maybe I am not trained in the medical profession, but neither am I stupid!

Al had a drainage tube at the site of the incision. Every two hours the nurses repositioned him. Almost every time, the drainage tube or the receptacle got caught under his body or his arm and I would have to free it so he would not be lying on it. How uncomfortable! Then I discovered that after drawing blood, the nurse almost always left the needle sheath in the bed, and I would find it under Al's leg where it would have already left an indentation.

As Al's hospital stay continued, the doctor advised that the NG tube gradually be discontinued. He gave instructions to the nurses for the tube to be clamped for two hours, then unclamped for four hours, clamped again for two hours, etc. As Al was able to tolerate the clamped times when food was given, they would see if he could indeed eat again. I was thrilled. This change meant that he was getting better!

The nurse came in and clamped the tube. I checked the time. After two hours, no one came to unclamp the tube. When I inquired of the next nurse who came into the room when they would be unclamping it, she said, "It doesn't need to be unclamped for at least another two hours." I tried to explain what the doctor had told me, but she disagreed and said that *she* had the orders and *she* would take care of it.

"I don't think you are listening!"

As I said, I may not have been trained in all of this, but I did know what the doctor said and I can tell time. It just so happened that earlier that afternoon, the director of nursing had dropped by and left her card saying if I ever needed anything I should call her. I felt it was time! *Lord, we have been here a long time, but this is the first time the director of nursing has visited us. You are such an on-time God. If she had come earlier, I may have misplaced her card. Thank You, Lord.*

She had already clocked out, but she took my call and came to the room. I explained the situation without whining. She listened intently then left the room to retrieve the chart from the nurses' station. Upon her return, she sat down and quietly read the doctor's orders.

She said, "You're right and I will take care of this immediately. Thank you for drawing it to my attention."

I begged her not to get me in trouble. "You know, I have to live here!" She assured me I would be safe. And I was. But from then on I never had any problems getting things done in a timely manner.

Al was in the hospital a total of twenty-eight days. I fed him, bathed him, dressed him, shaved him, brushed his teeth, and changed his linens. I stayed with him continually and loved him back to health. His doctor was wonderful to cheer us with words of encouragement. I was inspired by a piece of jewelry he wore, a silver cross with the cutout of a dove in the center. It spoke peace in the midst of the suffering.

Lord, what could I have done differently? How could I have provided more help? Have I forgiven the one who snapped at me? Have I learned anything through this? Will I do better next time?

Unfortunately, the vomiting did not stop. But at least we knew the stones were gone.

CHAPTER SIX

SEVEN STITCHES

*O*nly an eighth of an inch separated the wound from the jugular vein. With the ongoing balance problem, Al fell against the china cabinet one day and cut his neck. A lot of bleeding resulted. I rushed him to the emergency room where they put in seven stitches. The doctor said we should be thankful the vein wasn't cut. And we were thankful.

Because they were extremely busy, I had been asked to leave the emergency room to wait until they finished with Al. He was still able to communicate fairly well at that time, so I decided if he needed me he would ask for me. So I waited. And waited. But no one came to let me know how things were going, if they were almost finished, if he was doing all right, or if he would be going home soon.

I wonder if something has gone wrong. Did he need further attention? Maybe the jugular vein was involved. Many questions ran through my head. Finally, I inquired at the desk in the waiting room why it was taking so long.

After checking, they said he couldn't go home yet because he had a fever. I waited some more. I asked if it would be all right for me to see him for just a few minutes. When I went into the curtained area where he lay, he seemed to be resting and not anxious, so I returned to the waiting room. More than five hours later, they said they would have to admit him.

Without too much difficulty, we got Al situated in a room. I stayed with him, of course, leaving only for a couple of minutes to dash down to the cafeteria before they closed to get a take-out. Before I left, I went to the nurses' station across the hall from his room and asked them to keep a close watch on him because he had a severe balance problem and could fall easily.

"Oh, sure, no problem," they assured me.

In the few minutes I was gone, I discovered that sure enough he had tried to get to the bathroom and fell. I suppose they heard him fall and quickly helped him get back into the bed. *Did I waste my breath? Were my expectations too high? Should I have gone without food and stayed with him? Were they listening at all?*

Then the doctors began to order tests. I wondered if this was because Al had just become eligible for Medicare the month before. It was suggested he had the flu. He was taking glucose intravenously, and they said his blood sugar was high, so they sent a dietitian to the room to educate me on foods that cause elevated blood sugar.

They sent a "swallow" expert because they noticed he had difficulty swallowing. Next a speech therapist came to evaluate him. Following that, they asked if he had sleep apnea. More testing. He ended up spending the night in the "sleep" room, all hooked up to wires and "leads" to determine his sleep patterns.

As I sat observing the procedure, the person in charge acted dizzy, as if she had just fallen off a merry-go-round. She talked to herself, asking and answering her own questions, reprimanding herself when she made a mistake. Some of the leads were to be "glued" onto the scalp, others clipped on, and still others used suction to adhere to his skin. She got the locations mixed up and had to take some off and replace them with the correct ones; then she couldn't seem to remember where the others should have been.

Should I report this seeming incompetence? Will the results of the test be valid?

Eventually, he was pronounced "wired" and the testing began. I stayed with him to keep him from trying to get up. Now if he would just go to sleep. After four hours, he still lay there wide awake. I tried singing softly to him. I recited Scripture quietly. What normally worked to help him go to sleep didn't work. Hours went by while he just looked around the room, looked at me, looked at the lady in the window, but no hint of sleepiness occurred.

Lord, You know we need You during this long night. Please help Al to relax and sleep so we can get this test finished.

At 4:45 a.m. he finally dozed off for about fifteen minutes. The dizzy lady behind the observation window declared it a "win" and began unhooking him. What kind of pattern could be traced in that brief length of time?

I don't remember how many different things they tested him for, but I suppose the fact that he now had Medicare had something to do with it. You didn't hear that from me. I did, however, ask when they were going to do a pregnancy test.

Al stayed in the hospital for a week for seven stitches.

CHAPTER SEVEN

THE MIRACLE

*A*l had a strange look on his face as if he were trying to decide something. We were at home just relaxing, watching television.

"What's wrong?" I asked, observing that he was taking his own pulse. When I stepped over to him and took it, it was 120. I called a dear friend who was a retired army nurse, described Al's symptoms, and asked her what I should do.

"He really needs to be seen by a doctor," she said emphatically.

This was a couple of years after the onset of Al's mysterious illness. Up to this point we had learned nothing about the cause of the illness or a diagnosis, and certainly no treatment was offered.

By this point Al was already having a very difficult time walking because of his lack of balance. It was a struggle to get him into the car. As I drove to the nearest hospital he simply sat next to me in silence. About fifteen minutes into the trip, I asked him what he would tell the doctor when we arrived.

He pointed to his chest and said, "Chest pains."

"Chest pains?" I shouted. "You didn't say anything about chest pains! When did *that* start?"

"Just a few minutes ago," he whispered.

I grabbed the steering wheel a little tighter and accelerated a wee bit over the speed limit. I reasoned, *If I get pulled over by the highway patrol, I'll simply ask them to escort me to the hospital–and step on it!*

At the emergency room the medical staff hooked Al up to an EKG very quickly. About 11 p.m. they finally told me they couldn't detect any problem, but they wanted to keep him for observation just to make sure they hadn't missed anything.

A friend from church was at the same hospital in the waiting room with one of his family members and heard the doctor's report. He made me promise that I would keep in touch and let him know what happened. I agreed.

Shortly thereafter, I learned that the hospital didn't have a room available, so they needed to transfer Al to a larger hospital in the next town about thirty-five minutes away. I agreed and said I would follow in my car, but they told me not to try to keep up with the ambulance. By then it was midnight and pouring down rain; I couldn't have kept up if I tried.

At the second hospital I hurried to the admissions desk, but the ER nurse intercepted me and called me back to emergency immediately. The doctor there pulled me aside and explained that during the trip to the hospital, Al's oxygen level dropped dangerously low, indicating a blood clot. The ambulance team called ahead and had the pulmonary doctor waiting. An ultrasound revealed that the entire right ventricle was filled with one huge blood clot. The ER doctor made a drawing of another clot resting across the top of his lungs where the bronchial tubes connect.

I stared blankly at the sketch. "What does this mean?"

He hesitated for a moment. "If the clot moves, it's over."

A young pulmonary doctor who had been working with Al said I needed to call in the family. I explained that his family members were scattered all across the country and no one was near enough to come.

Al lay on the gurney, fully conscious but in pain. The pulmonary doctor cautioned him emphatically, "Al, don't move! Don't even scratch your nose! If the clot moves, you will die."

The doctor said it was all right for me to talk to him, but not to let him move. I bent over Al, looking into his blue eyes, and asked if he was aware of the gravity of what the doctor had said.

"Yes," he said, "but it's okay; God isn't finished with me yet."

The pulmonary doctor approached me with more news. "Only one in ten thousand survives this."

My mouth went dry, my heart rate accelerated, and my knees went weak all at the same time. Even I knew those were not very good odds. I glanced at Al, who was of course listening, being careful not to move. My entire being tried to process this whole development. *Think, Lois! Think!* Somehow I was able to formulate a sentence to ask if anything could be done.

My mind whirled. *God, is this how it will all end? Is it Your will that Al should die now? Are You here?*

After hesitating, the pulmonary doctor answered, "Only one thing. . ." And he hesitated again. "But I can't say it will necessarily work." He explained they would put in four IVs and administer mega-doses of heparin to thin the blood.

O God! There is a shred of hope! You are the God of miracles! Please, God, show us what to do.

"If he were your brother, what would you do?" I asked.

He immediately replied, "I'd go for it."

I nodded. "Let's do it!"

The ER staff had been on standby at attention throughout our brief conversation, ready to spring into action. Orders were quickly and succinctly given. They allowed me to stay in the room while they hooked Al up and in a matter of minutes started the IVs.

They explained to me that he could die at any moment and therefore I didn't have to leave. They continued to work with him. *What does one do when one's beloved lifetime sweetheart is facing imminent death? Why can't I think? Why can't I pray? What should I be doing?*

I knew I had to stay out of their way, but my arms wanted to hold him; I wanted to be by his side, touching him. By then it was after 2:30 a.m. They admonished him over and over not to move. He seemed to understand and complied with their commands.

Two compassionate nurses escorted me to a comfort room to explain the seriousness of the situation and to help me through the existing crisis. One prayed with me. *Please let me go back to Al. What if he dies and I'm not there with him?* It's hard to remember what took place because my mind was on what was happening to Al and worrying if he was okay.

One nurse asked if she could make any calls for me. I couldn't concentrate on who needed to be notified. I remembered my promise and called the friend who had seen us at the first hospital and asked to be notified if we needed him. If ever there was a time, it was now.

Of course, at 3:30 in the morning, I awakened him, but he said, "I'm on my way!" It seemed like hours. *O God, don't leave me now!* He called a mutual friend and by 4:30 they arrived.

Meanwhile, the nursing staff offered me coffee, food, anything–but that was the furthest thing from my mind. The only thought I could verbalize was, "Just take me back to Al."

After he was hooked up to the four IVs, they took Al to ICU. When I hurried in, Al saw me but was careful not to turn his head. They stationed me beside his bed with strict instructions to make sure he did not cross his legs or move in any way. What a mission! Who could sleep!

The friends who had arrived were allowed to come into the ICU for just a brief moment. They prayed over Al and went to the waiting room. Just knowing they were there, and praying, was so comforting.

The weary pulmonary doctor, who had worked all day and was now working all night, came in a number of times throughout what was left of the night to check on Al. He would just stand and stare at the monitors, then leave and return again about half an hour later. He never left the hospital.

About seven o'clock in the morning the doctor walked in and once again silently stared at the monitors. But this time a faint hint of a smile played across his lips. The numbers were up! The oxygen level had increased ever so slightly, but it was enough to bring a look of relief to his face and rejuvenate his sleep-deprived body. The heparin was working! I joined him in thanking God. What a relief! But Al was a long way from being well.

About that time the doctor who saw Al at the first hospital paid an unprecedented visit to the ICU to check on Al. Simultaneously, four friends arrived who had heard about Al. Apparently the personnel in charge of allowing visitors had been instructed to give anyone and everyone permission to come to the ICU because Al was not expected to live. After a brief consultation with the pulmonary doctor, the visiting doctor asked us to join hands to make a circle around Al's bed as he led in prayer. He knew and we knew that prayer was the only thing that would save Al. Even though my mind was in a fog and my thinking impaired, I was grateful.

One of the friends who came to visit went to the department store and bought me some fresh clothes and a toothbrush. Only after I had been assured it was all right for me to leave Al's side did I go to the adjacent restroom about ten steps away to clean up. A friend offered to keep vigil and promised not to allow Al to move. I rivaled the speed of Superman in changing and was back in a flash!

A steady stream of our caring friends came and went, offering encouragement and prayers. Days and nights melted into each other as Al remained in critical condition in the ICU. I wouldn't leave his side.

Eventually his condition stabilized and he was moved to a room. A Greenfield Vena Cava Filter was inserted to prevent any future blood clots from passing through to his heart and lungs.

Hospital staff members and personnel covering the ER the night Al was admitted came to his room to see the "miracle man." In our follow-up visits to the pulmonary doctor, they continued to remark about the impossible situation they had witnessed. Al's statement kept ringing in my ears: "It's all right; God isn't finished with me yet." Apparently, He wasn't.

What a victory when the doctor deemed Al well enough to come home! We loaded him into the car and off we went. *Home.* It sounded so good.

A dear friend in Florida felt impressed to drive up and be there with us when Al was released. She came to the hospital, got the house key, and timed it so that when we arrived home, the roast she had cooking in the oven produced the most wonderful aroma throughout the house. We both thought we *had* died and gone to heaven! What a delicious meal.

She cooked, cleaned, did laundry, ran errands, and shielded us from the constant yet greatly appreciated phone calls and visits. I had gone for days with only very short catnaps at Al's bedside. The uninterrupted rest was welcome. Our friend stayed an entire week, and what a blessing she was.

Lord, You always provide. Now I pray that her harvest of blessing will be abundant for giving of herself to us. How could we have survived without You? What would we have

*done without the many fervent prayers lifted in Al's behalf ?
We know it was only a miracle that brought him through this
terrible ordeal. Thank You, God, for Your divine intervention.*

Yes, Al finally came home, but he never walked again.

CHAPTER EIGHT

GOD'S PLAN

"*A*re you not hearing me? How am I supposed to get him into the house? Listen to me!*"

Real estate agents, in spite of my explicit instructions that there could be no steps or stairs, took me to various houses that had both. I have discovered that agendas affect their hearing. Most of the time it wasn't even necessary to get out of the car.

Retirement meant many things had to change. Suddenly we had a deadline to vacate the parsonage where we had lived for over seven years. In a small town, how many suitable places are available? We had to start somewhere.

Riding up and down the streets to look at houses didn't seem to be the right approach, but pictures in the real estate ads were so deceiving. Calling, looking, making appointments—it was all so laborious and time was running out. One house we thought we had settled on, right up to signing a contract, counter offers, etc., didn't pan out.

Al and I had made a "contract" with God that even if it was one penny more than a certain amount, we would know it was not the right thing to accept the offer. The seller came within $500. The broker was ecstatic. But we declined the offer. She and the seller's broker, whose mouths dropped open at our negative answer, offered to give up their commissions in order to "put us into our dream home."

"No," I said, "you don't understand. We have a higher contract that supersedes an earthly contract that we cannot break, and I couldn't expect you to understand that." We learned later what an enormous mistake we avoided by not succumbing to a seemingly wonderful situation.

Then we found a house that was a real dream. We could rent it at a very low price. It had a beautiful view of the city and the distant mountains, with perfect everything. The owner even asked if she could leave her patio furniture in the "four seasons" room. What a blessing!

Just one day before we were to sign a contract, and only twelve days before we had to vacate our present home, she changed her mind. *Now what? Where will we go? What should we do now?*

Another house was available, but it needed a ramp. The owner said he would rent it to us and build us a ramp. I thought of Rebekah in the Bible when Isaac's servant was wife-scouting for his master (Genesis 24:12). His criteria in choosing a bride was, "If I ask the prospective bride to give me a drink and she offers to water my camels also, I'll know she is the right person." And that's exactly what happened. In our case, however, two days later the owner changed his mind.

By that time I felt like the children of Israel when they had mountains on either side, the Red Sea in front of them, and Pharaoh's army chasing from behind. *Lord, HELP!*

The closer we got to the cutoff day, the more we prayed and wondered what the Lord had in mind. *What is He up to? What should we do? Should we rent a furnished cabin at the marina until we can find something? Should we move out of town?*

A friend from church called and said a woman who owned a rental house was having to evict her renters. "Would you be interested in looking at it?" At that point, we would have looked at a DOGHOUSE!

We drove eight-tenths of a mile out of the main part of town toward the lake to a little one-bedroom house . . . that had steps. My heart sank. However, the rest of the house seemed perfectly suitable.

The same day, a childhood friend in Illinois called and asked if we needed a ramp. She and her husband had purchased a rental house that had a ramp they would not be using. When I asked what the "drop" was, she said she would go measure it and call me back.

Meanwhile, I grabbed my trusty tape measure and dashed out to the prospective property and measured both front porch steps and back steps. Both were nineteen and a half inches from the base to the top of the steps. When my friend called back she said it was—yes, you guessed it—nineteen and a half inches!

Thank You, God! You have had this house sitting here all along; we just had to find it. You see, it was not vacant when we first started looking. God had to give the others time to get out! And my friend did not have the ramp. Sometimes we have to wait for God to work out the details, but He always does. "Wait for the Lord; take courage, and He will give strength to your heart; yes, wait for the Lord" (Psalm 27:14).

Another necessary detail we found was a large enough bathroom to accommodate the wheelchair and doors wide enough to allow the wheelchair to pass. Believe it or not, some of the houses we looked at were more than three times the size of this one and the bathrooms and doorways were too small and/or too narrow and wouldn't work for us.

My friends loaded the ramp onto a flatbed trailer and hauled it almost five hundred miles, put it up to the porch steps, slid it between the handrails of the steps, and presto—we were in business! The design and color perfectly matched the porch. No one would ever believe they had not been built at the same time. It left only the space of a sheet of paper between the porch handrails and the ramp handrails.

How could this happen? Was it a coincidence? Was it luck? Absolutely not!

Inside the little refurbished house, beautiful hardwood floors accommodated the wheelchair as did the wide doors and large bathroom. This house was built in the 1950s with us in mind! Two small bedrooms had been made into one and provided room for our queen-sized bed, both of us, *and* the wheelchair.

CHAPTER NINE

NEAR FATAL MISTAKE

"*I*sn't there some kind of medicine that would ease the pain Al suffers? Can't you give him *something* to make his life a little easier? Not to be drugged, but to take the edge off the unbearable pain?" I asked each professional who cared for Al.

We asked the doctor if he could prescribe something strong and fast-acting to help us cope with these episodes of pain. One drug he suggested was to be titrated to a level where it would relieve his pain somewhat, but Al would have to take it all the time. We decided against that; unfortunately nothing else was offered.

Al and I were invited to dinner with pastor friends who lived an hour away. Because of the pain, travel for Al was difficult. During a scheduled visit with the RN from Home Health we discussed the ongoing pain issue. It seemed that no medication would alleviate the acute attacks of severe and extended bouts of pain. He was unable to describe the pain or even its exact location.

"Oh," said the RN confidently, "I can fix that. I can put a pain patch on him today that will work for seventy-two hours. Tonight, put on this additional patch. By the time you go to your dinner occasion, he should be fine."

A perfect example of cookie-cutter treatment.

I suppose we were desperate and her explanation sounded pretty good. So we agreed and allowed her to put on the patch. That night, I placed the second patch on his other shoulder as she had indicated. However, the next morning as I gave Al his bed bath, I noticed his breathing had slowed. He didn't wake up even though I turned him back and forth, dressing him in bed, then tried to wake him to eat. Still I got no response. The only thing different from the day before was the patch, so I removed one of them.

I called the doctor and gave him details of the symptoms and the name of the patch. He was alarmed.

"Who put that on him?" he asked, raising his voice.

Not waiting for a reply, he almost shouted into the phone, "Call 911! You get an ambulance immediately! I'll call the hospital where he has been admitted before and give the emergency staff instructions on what to do as soon as he arrives. Hurry!" He slammed down the phone.

What a shock. I made the 911 call, and in the short time I waited for the ambulance my mind raced as I tried to think of things I needed to do to close up the house and be ready to go to the hospital. Al was completely out.

When the ambulance arrived, I gave them the doctor's orders with the name and location of the hospital. The driver stopped the gurney in the middle of the room, planted his feet, and refused to move Al onto the gurney.

"What's the problem?" I asked, puzzled at his behavior.

Protesting loudly that he would have to pass another hospital in order to get to the one the doctor recommended, he declared, "I'm not allowed to do that."

I replied, "Please, just do as the doctor has ordered."

"Ma'am, you don't understand; I could lose my job."

I exploded, "And I could lose my husband! Just do it!"

It became a standoff. This was not the time to play games. What authority did I have? What were my rights? I looked at Al in his almost comatose condition and screamed to the driver, "I'll pay for it–just go!"

He was still reluctant but finally agreed and loaded Al onto the gurney. "However," he continued in a threatening tone, "if he develops a problem on the way, I will have to stop at the nearest hospital."

What could I do but agree and pray that he would get to the designated hospital? ER staff were awaiting our arrival and quickly went into action. They rushed Al to intensive care and started treatment immediately. For four days he fought his way back to consciousness. I set up vigil at his bedside and waited and prayed. Because of Al's inability to communicate, I was allowed to stay with him.

I realize that others may not have the same reaction to the patch, but again I had to be the watchdog and make sure the medication administered was safe for Al. This time it was not. Trusting others to "try" certain treatments can be very dangerous. I learned that I must remain alert to any and all changes.

Thank You, God, that I was perceptive in this situation. I want to always "trust in the Lord with all my heart and lean not to my own understanding" (Proverbs 3:5).

CHAPTER TEN

ACQUIRING A HANDICAP VAN

"*M*ost people are not aware that a lot of unclaimed money is out there that belongs to people just like you!" the automated phone messenger hawked. "And for a mere $28.50 we will disclose the amount of your new-found wealth."

Don't you know we jumped at the chance and rushed to the phone to stake our claim!

Hold that thought.

Maybe I should start at the beginning. When it became necessary for Al to be in a wheelchair all the time, I had to transfer him from the chair to the car seat whenever we traveled anywhere. Then I would fold up the wheelchair and hoist it into the trunk of the car.

At our destination, I had to heave the wheelchair out of the trunk, put Al into it, and wheel him into the church, restaurant, or wherever we were going. Lifting a normal wheelchair in and out of the trunk was a challenge, so I began to look for a lighter-weight model to carry in the trunk for away-from-home activities. Even though I am a former farm girl with strong arms and a strong back, it was still difficult.

One of our friends who is a women's conference speaker heard about our need. At her next speaking engagement, she presented to the audience her goal to collect enough money to purchase a lightweight chair for us. That very day, in that one offering, the ladies gave the total amount to the very dollar for the chair. We bought the lighter chair immediately. What a blessing! It surely helped save my back. Now, by carrying the lighter chair in the trunk, it was easily lifted out, used, and then afterward replaced in the trunk.

Another friend in Illinois heard of a handicap van being sold by someone in her church. She put us in touch with the seller, and we made arrangements to purchase the vehicle sight unseen. Caring friends delivered it to Tennessee. What a wonderful design! A ramp that descended from the side of the van could automatically be engaged with the press of a button. We were then able to wheel Al right up the ramp and into the van. No more lifting heavy wheelchairs!

To purchase this amazing van, we had to put up our car as collateral, borrow from the credit union, and basically contribute all financial resources available. With Al's rapid physical deterioration, it was not a luxury, it was a necessity. Attempts failed to sell our top-of-the-line car that was loaded with extras, even though it was priced to sell.

Lord, why will this car not sell? You know we need the extra money to purchase the van.

Then it became evident to me through times of praying that the Lord wanted me to *give* the car to a certain couple in ministry who desperately wanted and needed the car but couldn't afford to buy it.

Lord, can we talk? You have asked my obedience in many instances and I have responded. You have asked me to give money to someone in need. You have directed me to buy someone's lunch or dinner, someone I didn't even know. You have told me to call a certain person at a specific time, sometimes someone I had not spoken to in months or even years, only to learn that the call was made at the perfect time. Your Spirit has urged me to go to a certain place, and when I got there I saw that it was Your hand of guidance in my life. And I remember the time You directed someone at church to place an offering in my hand surreptitiously, and I rejoiced that You had met a specific need we were praying about. Then, within the hour, You asked me to give it away. No, I didn't understand because I felt what I imagine Abraham felt when You asked him to sacrifice the long-awaited promised heir (Genesis 22). But I obeyed. Then You replaced the exact amount two days later from another source. It seemed easy to obey You in all of those situations, but this? This is different! This is major! This is out of my comfort zone. How do I know this is Your leading?

What an inward struggle! We had no salaries. No ongoing resources were available except Social Security. But in seeking God, I knew that He wanted my obedience. *But why this way? Who would help us if God didn't come through?*

He directed me to Luke 6:38: "Give, and it will be given unto you–good measure, pressed down, shaken together, and running over will they pour into your lap." In the Greek, "lap" is used in place of the King James Version word "bosom," which is made by pulling up the skirt hem forming a large pocket for carrying things.

How much clearer could He make it? I settled it in my heart. I was willing.

I explained to Al the best I could that God was speaking to me. He said I had better do as I felt the Lord directing me. So we invited the couple over without disclosing the reason why we wanted them to come. We joyfully presented them with the key and the title to the luxury car. They were stunned, but we knew we were walking in obedience.

Absolutely nothing was said; no one knew we gave the car away. Until this book becomes available, they still don't know. But suddenly money began to come from everywhere. It was amazing! For example, I came home one day to find a lovely "Thinking of You" card containing five one-hundred-dollar bills. Checks came in the mail from people we hardly knew, confessing that they didn't know why they were sending the money, they just knew they should. One unusual source involved something almost unbelievable. Then came the automated phone call, which, by the way, we promptly ignored.

About two weeks later a real person called and asked our full names and birth dates, but before answering I interrupted her and asked the nature of the call. She explained that she was with an agency (and gave the name of it) whose job it was to help locate people who had monies outstanding that could be claimed.

"We have already received a call a couple of weeks ago telling us the same thing. No, thank you," I said, and was ready to hang up. She quickly assured me that they were not associated with any other company and that they had been trying to locate us for some time. The conversation ensued back and forth as I continued to declare my skepticism and she continued to declare her legitimacy and authenticity.

She asked if we had ever lived in Atlanta. I answered yes. Then she asked for the last four digits of Al's Social Security number. I had been well trained in previous situations to never give out Social Security numbers or credit card numbers.

"NO WAY!"

She responded that it was all right because she already had it.

She offered me a phone number of the Better Business Bureau to check her legitimacy.

"Ha," I snorted, "it's probably your neighbor's phone number, and she is a co-conspirator; then you'll split the money with her. And, by the way, how does your company make its money to pay your salary?"

She was unruffled. "We get 10 percent of the amount matched with the recipient."

I wasn't convinced. "Where is this money supposed to

be located? How much is it?"

Of course, she was not allowed to tell me that. Yeah, right!

Again and again she tried to reassure me that she wanted to help me. I had to admit she knew a lot about us. I finally said I would think about it and call her back. She didn't hesitate to give me her phone number. We hung up. I sat there with the phone in my hand, bewildered and wondering. *Lord, You heard that; what shall I do? Why couldn't I have been born smart instead of beautiful?*

Within a few minutes the phone rang. It was the same woman.

"Mrs. Mimbs, I have taken another look at this situation and discovered that because this money is considered government money, we will not be able to take out 10 percent. So you will receive the entire amount. I just thought I should let you know that."

"Trust in the Lord with all your heart and lean not on your own understanding; in all your ways acknowledge Him and He shall direct your paths" (Proverbs 3:5-6). *All right, Lord, You will have to direct me. I trust You with all my heart.* I finally agreed to allow her to contact the entity who supposedly held these funds, hoping and praying it wasn't a scam.

Within a short time a man called to verify all the information to make sure that we were who we claimed to be. I explained my hesitancy, and he said he understood.

Then he let down his guard and spoke with emotion. "We are so glad to locate you. We have been trying to reach you for a number of years!" He stated that each time they tried to contact us at the former address, their mail was always returned.

We certainly had left a forwarding address, but apparently it expired before they needed it. I believe God had our future in His hands and "kept" the money there "for such a time as this" (Esther 4:14b).

As the mystery unfolded we had to acknowledge that it was truly a God thing. While we lived in Atlanta, Al had purchased several IRAs to take care of taxes owed and had forgotten about it. The interest had grown and matured it.

The man further stated that if we would wait just three more days, the interest would compound again. *Hey, what's a few more days? We didn't even know we had the money!*

He made arrangements to transfer the funds to us. Are you ready for this? The final amount was more than the price we had asked for the car we gave away! We were blessed in addition to blessing the other couple in their need.

Not only was it a tremendous financial blessing, but also a learning and stretching experience that increased our faith to believe God for even greater things, financially and otherwise. Praise God from whom all blessings flow! *Lord, I apologize; I suppose I am a slow learner!*

CHAPTER ELEVEN

LORD, I MISS THE OLD AL

*A*t the onset of his illness Al could still communicate, but as the months went by, sometimes his thoughts would get jumbled. Laymen of the congregation were very helpful to fill in with the preaching on his really bad days. Unfortunately, the bad days were coming closer and closer together. Testing, therapy, doctor visits—but none of it yielding any answers. Bouncing from one place to another, we actually felt no one took the time or effort to help us because they simply didn't know *what* to do. His symptoms were out of the box.

Al loved to go to church. He insisted on being dressed in a suit, white shirt, tie, and belt just to sit in the wheelchair. Why not? He was a whole person, just as he had always been, except now he couldn't walk. Sometimes I begged him to skip the belt. I chided, "I promise, your pants won't fall off." But he wouldn't hear of it. We had to put on a belt.

One young couple asked him to perform their wedding ceremony. I reminded them that he would have to do it from his wheelchair. But they didn't mind–they wanted Al to marry them.

I typed out on cards each part of the ceremony, each thing he had to say. The day of the wedding, some strong guys lifted Al onto the platform at church and wheeled him into position. Then I assisted him, sitting by his side and handing him the correct cards at the appropriate times.

It was a first. And it was a last, the last wedding Al performed.

For several months after this Al had a gradual decline in his speaking vocabulary. It was hardly noticeable at first because on bad days he slept a lot and barely communicated. I understood. So when he did speak it was like manna from heaven. On one of our trips to the doctor's office, I looked over at Al, admiring his recent haircut and his favorite shirt that enhanced his blue eyes. "You look so good I could eat you with a spoon," I quipped. "Will you marry me?" He gave me a deadpan look. "No, I'm already married." I loved his surprise responses.

"Good morning" was no longer there to greet the nurse. Shaking him gently by the shoulders would eventually evoke a "yes" or a "no" or "quit!" No cajoling or prodding could produce a desired response.

At mealtime, if I asked him to voice a preference for certain foods, he just sat with his head down, eyes closed, and no response.

Each time I answered the phone I would put it on speaker so he could hear the entire conversation. Usually the caller would say, "Tell Al we said hello." I quickly interrupted and told them he could hear them. Then the caller conversed directly with him, and he would respond with "Thank you," "How are you?" or "I'm fine."

I enjoyed keeping up with friends' birthdays. He and I would practice singing "Happy Birthday," then call the person and sing a duet for them.

When Al's sisters in Arizona and California called to check on him, it was usually no problem for him to respond to them. But for a number of months he did not respond at all even though they gave him numerous opportunities and options, sometimes a question and sometimes a joke.

If I asked him if he was comfortable, warm, cold, tired, hungry, thirsty–there was no response. Our lifetime bedtime routine has always been to kiss goodnight and say "I love you," but he began to turn his head and wouldn't look at me, completely silent. My spirit was crushed, my heart ached, and my tears flowed. I felt as if I had lost the love of my life. *Lord, please, PLEASE restore his speech.* More tears, more questions. *Peace, Lord, peace in the silent storm.*

When Bible study people came into our home each Tuesday, they would speak to Al. And always, heretofore, he responded with "Hi, how are you?" Then gradually nothing. I tried to assess the situation. *Did he have a slight stroke that took his ability to speak? Is he being obstinate? Is he still in there? Doesn't he understand? Is he receiving, but not sending?*

For many months I prayed for Al's speech to be restored. One week a man from the Bible study told Al goodbye as he was leaving, and Al said, "Bye." Oh, what rejoicing! A few days later he said "Morning" to the nurse. More rejoicing!

A few nights later, in February 2011 at bedtime, as I kissed him I told him I loved him. He looked at me, studying my face for a long time. Nothing. I begged him. I just needed to hear him tell me.

"Please tell me you love me!" I waited. "Please?" Then he took a deep breath, and with much struggle and hesitation, searching my face as if he could glean some help from me, he clearly verbalized, "I . . . love . . . you."

HALLELUJAH! Tears of joy flowed unchecked as I fell across him, hugging him, kissing him, thanking him, and repeating it back to him. "I love you, I love you, I love you, darling. Thank you for telling me!"

A little thing? Maybe. But it meant the world to me.

"Trust in the Lord and do good; inhabit the land and practice faithfulness. Have your delight in the Lord and he will give you the desires of your heart" (Psalm 37:3-4).

CHAPTER TWELVE

STRANDED!

*T*he heavy rain had passed but it was still drizzling as Al and I made our way across the parking lot of a large department store. Pushing Al's chair with my right hand and dragging the full shopping cart behind me with the left, taking care not to run over my heels, we dashed toward the van in the handicap space. I unlocked the door with my remote. But when I tried to engage the ramp, I noticed a bit of hesitation. Eventually it lowered and I pushed Al's chair up the ramp and fastened him into the EZ-lock.

After transferring my groceries into the van and returning the cart to the outdoor chute, we prepared to leave. I put the key into the ignition but nothing happened. The sound of silence was devastating. Now what? I got out and opened the hood. Don't ask me why because I surely didn't know how to diagnose a motor problem. I might as well have been looking at brain surgery! Well, maybe if the battery cables were corroded I would know *that*.

May I digress? Three times the van totally stopped on us, two times in 95-degree heat with no way to get Al out of the van. By the time the wrecker transported it to the garage, it would start and appear to be all right. Three different garages couldn't diagnose the problem and therefore declared it all right to drive. Two of the places each kept it for over a week!

"We have checked everything, and we've driven it over and over and had no problems with it. Just go ahead and drive it, and if you break down again just call us."

The people at these repair shops didn't seem to understand that when the power went down on the vehicle, it was disabled as far as opening windows, operating the ramp, and of course running the air conditioning.

Even well-meaning friends, upon hearing of our breakdown, stated vehemently, "Why didn't you *call* me; I would have come and gotten you." But almost no one had a vehicle that could accommodate the wheelchair and Al. Because he had no use of his legs, I was unable to transfer him into another car. Plus, the wheelchair didn't fold, so it would not fit in most cars. Maybe a pickup truck would work. I could just see us riding down the highway with our hair blowing and bugs sticking in our teeth as we wound our way home in the back of a truck. Also remember we would first have to get Al and the chair into the truck! Now, mind you, I'm not looking a gift horse in the mouth, okay?

On this particular day, a kind-looking man passed by with his grocery cart, so I called out to him. "What's wrong?" he asked as he came our way. He jiggled the cables of the battery and checked other things. It began to rain harder. An elderly lady walked by and gawked. She asked if we needed an umbrella, but not waiting for an answer, promptly went to her car and brought back a huge golf umbrella, opened it, and held it over the man who was checking the van motor. She left a few minutes later but said we could keep her umbrella. Did an angel drop out of the sky?

The nice man finally declared the battery dead even though it had been only a few months since I'd replaced it. I decided we needed a wrecker. Cell phone to the rescue. Meanwhile, the man gave me the number of the handicap van service. It was five o'clock in the afternoon and I was already thinking, *I'll bet they've quit running by this time of day.*

When I reached their office, the dispatcher wasn't sure she could get anyone but said she would call me back. I pleaded with her to do her best and told her my desperate situation. When she called back after what seemed like forever, they were getting ready to close, but she said she had one driver who was an hour away. Caught in a bad storm and unable to see in the downpour, she had to pull over to the side of the road. However, if we could wait, she would have that driver come and get us. I thought, *What's an hour among friends?* We had no other recourse!

Since the ramp quit working in the down position, I was able to remove Al from the van and take him back into the department store to wait and to watch for the handicap van. I began to be concerned about Al's Foley catheter. Would it hold out until we got home? He had not had any lunch. If I left my lookout position, I might miss the van coming to pick us up. Al's nose was running constantly and I had just used the last Kleenex. *Lord?* Wouldn't you know, He answered before I called.

A sweet young couple had observed earlier that we were having car trouble and approached us just inside the store where we were waiting. "Is there anything we can do to help you?" Goodness, yes! The man stayed and talked with us while she went and got some tissues and a pack of crackers for Al. How grateful we were for their kindness! Hundreds of folks passed by us and never even glanced our way. But God provided help at the right time. He's Jehovah Jireh, our Provider.

While we were waiting, the wrecker service called and said they had gone to a store by the same name fifteen miles in the opposite direction, but when the driver didn't find us there he left and was now halfway back to his original starting position and would soon be at our location.

Oh my! Were my communication skills going haywire? What did I say? By this point we had been waiting two hours.

Just about that time the handicap van pulled up–at the wrong door. All the waving and yelling didn't faze the driver. She went in at the other entrance. And we waited. Sure enough, she finally realized that she needed to try the other door. *Did you not hear me? Or is it again my communication skills gone awry? Another page in my book. No one listens anymore!*

She was so kind we couldn't be mad at her. Drivers of the handicap vans have to go through a lot to load a passenger into their vehicle. She had just been through a terrible storm and, as we found out later, had been up since 4:30 that morning to get someone to the hospital for tests. Just as she was loading Al and I was loading the groceries, the wrecker came chugging up the parking lot. The rain had stopped and out came the hot sun. *Thank You, Lord. Your timing is perfect!*

Our van went one way on the flatbed truck and we went home in the handicap van—starving and tired, but with a little more experience under our belts.

CHAPTER THIRTEEN

NOT AGAIN!

"*O*h no! What's happening? The motor is cutting out! I have no power!"

For several years following the purchase of our handicap van, we had trouble-free transportation. We drove several thousand miles on both short and long trips without experiencing any difficulties. Traveling mercies abounded, for which I am so very thankful. Then we had a few hitches. Experience has taught me that garages and mechanics often view a woman customer as an opportunity to make some money. So when difficulties began to arise with the van, I approached the incidents with great caution. But our trouble doubled.

To you fellows, this is elementary, I know. But for those readers who are not mechanically inclined, I will put the cookies on the bottom shelf. Whenever the electrical system of our van shut down, because there was no power to operate anything, we were basically stuck.

In our travels, we often took a delightful longtime friend with us. She rode in another wheelchair on the passenger side while Al's chair was secured behind and slightly to the right of my driver's seat. I told her that her job was to entertain me and keep me awake as I drove. Laughing, talking, and singing together helped so much on long trips.

On this particular day we followed behind other family members on our way to attend a funeral just outside of Atlanta. As we headed down Interstate 85 nearing our exit ramp, the motor began to cut out. *O Lord! Please help us! We have plenty of gas, and no warning lights are on–what is wrong?* We limped off the interstate and coasted just past the lane of traffic feeding into the city traffic. The motor was totally dead. Turning the key in the ignition yielded a sickening complete silence. We were facing the sun in 90-degree weather at five o'clock in the afternoon in rush-hour traffic. Almost instantly, I began to "dew," as we say in the South. It's unladylike to sweat or perspire. I tried letting the windows down. Nothing. Opening the doors a little provided only a minimal amount of air, but at least we could breathe.

Our lead car didn't realize we were no longer following. Cell phones to the rescue! I called and we agreed that they should go on to the funeral home; we would try to make it later.

At that moment a wrecker was leaving a business adjacent to our location in the street. He stopped and offered help, but he was already loaded so he said he would be back in about twenty minutes. *By then I will have expired into a puddle.* We thanked him and waited.

Almost immediately another wrecker came up and stopped next to our van. A very nice driver jumped out and came to my window (that could not be let down). I opened the door. The dilemma escalated during our brief conversation because, first of all, he could not tow us with passengers in the van since it is against the law (remember, the ramp would not go down in order to get Al out of the van), and two, neither could he put the van on the flatbed with passengers inside it.

While we talked, another wrecker came alongside us. Are you keeping track? We are up to three wreckers at this point. *This* driver suggested I take the van out of gear and let it roll back down a steep hill right beside us that went into a large car dealership where they had garage service. Can you visualize that? You very well know I jumped at the chance! Instead, as I stepped out of the van, I graciously offered to allow *him* to back it down the steep hill. Remember, the van had no power for steering or brakes or anything!

Al and our friend had to remain in the van because the ramp was disabled. "Here we go!" They had the ride of their lives going backwards down a steep hill, sliding to a stop right at the entrance of the dealership. My friend told me later she covered her eyes, held her breath, and prayed!

Meanwhile, in the middle of the traffic the *second* wrecker driver escorted me to his wrecker to give me a ride down the hill. As I approached the door of his mega-truck in my high heels and silk dress, which by now was sticking to me, I observed that my nose was level with the bottom of the cab door. Bewildered, I turned to look at the driver. I could tell by the amused expression on his face that he knew what I was thinking. He smiled and assured me that he would help me get up into the cab. The bottom step looked doable, along with help from a very long handle located beside the door. So I grabbed the handle, took the biggest midair split I have ever taken, and with the truck driver giving me a shove was able to make the first step in my ascent into his truck cab. Whew! Only two more steps to go! *Hey, I was getting good at this.* Once inside the cab I plunked down onto the seat, pulled the skirt of my sweaty silk dress inside, and the door was shut.

I was aghast as we drove down the steep hill with all things intact. What must it have been like to be freewheeling it in our disabled van? No, thank you!

Meanwhile, the other guy who had bravely commandeered the van backwards down the steep hill was waiting for us at the bottom. We thanked him profusely. What a feat! Approaching the outdoor desk, we found everyone from secretary to management tremendously accommodating.

Someone from the service department came and raised the hood. Within seconds he discovered the electrical problem, so they bypassed it long enough to lower the ramp to let Al and our friend out into the breezeway. Several guys then pushed the van into a bay for repair.

This could take hours! I called Al's niece who I knew had access to a handicap van. We were able to have her and her husband come to our rescue we thought. When they arrived about thirty minutes later, we discovered that the EZ-lock was under the driver's seat. There was no place to fasten Al's chair into the floor. It would be much too dangerous to drive without securing him. Plan B didn't work.

Did God want to show His glory and provision? Was I impatient, trying to figure things out on my own? "Wait for the Lord, and take courage, and He will give strength to your heart" (Psalm 27:14).

The dealership staff ushered the three of us into an air-conditioned waiting room and gave us cold water. After broiling in the hot sun in our dress clothes, we eagerly welcomed the refreshment.

Meanwhile, my thoughts raced. *Lord, will I need to get a loan to pay for these repairs? It is so near closing time, they may need to keep the van overnight. We are miles from our hotel. Lord, do You know where we are and how long this will take? What about the funeral visitation? God, I have to put this into Your hands and trust You. Thank You for being my peace.*

We met some interesting people in the waiting room. Conversation included praising God for His goodness for providing the repair place precisely at the location of our breakdown. Of course, we may never know His real purpose for our being there at that particular time, but we did not fail to give Him praise. At least we were temporarily safe.

In what seemed like a very short time, the repairman came to let us know that our vehicle was ready. *What? Ready?*

How can that be? They assured us they had test-driven the van twice and everything was fine. By then it was after six o'clock. *They will probably charge us overtime!* Now the moment of truth: the cost. I found myself holding my breath. The receptionist tapped a few keys on the computer, wrote down some figures. *How bad is it?*

"All right," she said, smiling, "that will be twenty dollars." TWENTY DOLLARS! I could hardly believe my ears. *Thank You, Lord, for Your mercy and for taking care of us when we did not know how to care for ourselves. Another divine blessing! Why do we doubt You?*

Driving out of the dealership with directions to the funeral home in our hand, we overflowed with gratitude in our hearts. Once again God had orchestrated the entire situation. "God is for us a refuge and a fortress; found to be a present help in time of trouble. Therefore, we do not fear. . ." (Psalm 46:1).

CHAPTER FOURTEEN

WE NEED A FIX

*W*hew! What a hot day!

We had just come from the doctor's office and needed to have a prescription filled before going home. Pulling into the parking space in front of the pharmacy, I quickly ran into the store, leaving Al asleep in the van with the air conditioning running.

When I came out about ten minutes later, the motor had stopped. *Oh no, not again.* I tried and tried to start the motor, but it just chugged. I sat there for awhile in the heat and waited. Then I tried again and it started. So I backed out carefully and headed for home. The motor wasn't running too well. But I continued to chug as long as it would move. We were only about a mile and a half from home so I hoped I could coax it into getting us there without having to call a wrecker again. One block from the pharmacy it quit dead as a doornail, with 97 degrees registering on the van thermometer.

Once again it was after five o'clock. But when I called the wrecker service they answered and said they would be right there. This time I made sure I communicated our correct location. As we waited the motor cooled down, so when the wrecker arrived to help us the driver asked me to try starting it. The motor hesitated, and I can't say it roared to life but it acted as if it was going to be resuscitated. The driver said he thought I could make it home all right. Are you kidding? No way! I had to cross the railroad tracks.

He smiled and promised he would follow behind very closely. *I can't believe I've been talked into doing this!* We choked and sputtered along, and as we approached the rail-road tracks I checked left and right very carefully to make sure the coast was clear. My emotions soared sky high. What if this thing stopped on the tracks? I gunned the motor and we made it across the tracks, through the major intersection, and then it died again.

The wrecker driver positioned his wrecker in front of the van and tilted the flatbed down so it formed a ramp. He attached the cables to the front of the van–which we still occupied. Our entire entourage was in the middle of the road in rush-hour traffic. He started pulling up the van with us inside. I white-knuckled the steering wheel and told Al to hold on. That last quarter of a mile, I felt as if we were at Six Flags. Talk about ridin' high! It was actually pretty scary.

The wrecker driver asked us not to tell anyone. Are you kidding? We were so grateful to be at home again and not broiling in the heat, I wouldn't rat on him if I had to. I don't recommend this type of transportation, but when desperation reigns it's easy to succumb to the quickest remedy available.

Our van was taken to two different very reputable repair shops where it lived for two weeks, and each place said they could not make it "act up." They declared it all right to drive. Oh sure. That's easy for you to say!

But once again, drive we did.

CHAPTER FIFTEEN

BREAKDOWN No. 3

*I*t seems the older I get, the younger everyone else becomes. Our new doctor looked as if he just stepped off the high school football field. I really did like the way he made eye contact the entire time we talked, but I was disappointed that he just looked at Al. He didn't touch him or speak to him. I have learned that the assumption goes like this: if he can't walk, he can't hear or understand or communicate. So all conversation happened above Al's head.

How shall I respond to this situation? Should I even address it? Can each of us picture ourselves in that wheelchair? Maybe I can understand what you are saying and maybe I can't. You don't know! At least give me the benefit of the doubt. I am still a person in this body, and I have feelings. Please don't ignore me.

I drove in silence ruminating over the events we had just experienced in the doctor's office.

On the way home, I stopped to get a much needed new phone. Al was asleep in his wheelchair, so leaving the motor running and the air conditioning on, I parked right in front of the store so I could see him from inside. (I know what you're thinking…don't you remember what happened the last time you did that?)

Before I continue, rewind to early that morning. I had

been praying about whether we should look for another vehicle. It was not good to be stranded on the highway with Al with no assistance available. So I prayed, "Lord, I've been asking You about purchasing another vehicle, and I suppose I haven't really been in earnest about it, so I'm asking that You show me today in a specific way whether we should be looking around for something else more reliable to drive."

When I came out of the store, the motor had cut off. It wouldn't start! After several attempts, I finally succeeded, and with the motor hesitating I once again backed out of the parking space. We made it down to the highway with the motor coughing and sputtering. (All you smart people, stay with me.)

Things seemed to be improving so I went through the light, turned left, and got onto the divided four-lane highway. Then it stalled in the middle of the road. The nightmare–or rather "daymare"–continued. I limped without power into a left turn lane in the median.

It was four o'clock in the afternoon, 95 degrees, and we were facing west. Sweat ran from every pore in my body. Al woke up, but I couldn't let the window down to allow some air in. I tried to explain to him what had happened.

Okay, we have been through this before. Pull out the trusty cell phone. Step one. The first order of business was to call the handicap van service to get someone to help me get Al home.

When the dispatcher answered she said, "Where are you?" I told her and she replied, "We don't have service there; that's in another county." So I asked her if she had a number available for the county I was in. "No, I don't, and I'm going to hang up now." *Lord, will You please help me to bless her and forgive her? Is this a test? Is this intended to conform me to the image of Your Son?*

As I searched my cell phone for numbers, a van pulled up beside me and a man got out and came to my door asking if he could help. He suggested various things to help me start the van. Nothing worked.

"I have to go right there to deliver these documents," he said, pointing to a building across the road, "but I'll be back to help you." I must admit, I wondered if he really would come back.

While he was gone, I called the wrecker service. "Please explain to your wife that we are not having an affair!" He laughed and said he would be there as soon as he could make the eighteen-mile trip.

The stranger not only returned but was carrying two cold drinks for us. What a blessing! He assessed the situation and said, "I can get your husband in my van." I explained that Al couldn't walk or stand, I was unable to lift him, and the wheelchair didn't fold.

He countered with the fact that he was in his work van and it did not have a backseat, so he felt certain we could leave Al in the chair and put the whole shebang into the back of his van.

What a nice fellow. Then my thoughts began to race. *What if he's an ax killer, looking for a victim? What if he's going to drive us into the lake?* Crazy stuff comes into your mind when it's 95 degrees and your brain is under duress.

While he was moving his tools and junk, I took my bill-fold and bag of items out of our van to transfer them into the front seat of his vehicle. Still wondering if this was a safe thing to do, I heard music from his radio tuned to a Christian station.

I called out over the back of the seat, "Are you a believer?"

"I surely am!" came the reply.

Whew! I felt better.

He coaxed our van to run long enough to let down the ramp. Then he wheeled Al around to the side door of his van and asked if I could now help him lift Al and the chair into the door. Piece o' cake! He suddenly decided to put a toolbox under his van doorway thinking we could do the lift in stages.

That sounded like a plan. But the wheels of the chair straddled the toolbox and it wedged there. We ended up picking up Al, the chair, *and* the full toolbox! Oh, my aching back.

"Bob" loaded us and had the chair tied down for safety. Yes, can you believe it? He even had tie-downs with him. Only wheelchair van owners have tie-downs. Wouldn't you say that confirmed God had all of this under His control? What were the odds that this entire scenario could have happened without the hand of God?

Just as we were ready to pull off for home, the wrecker service arrived. *Again, thank You, Lord. Your timing is perfect.*

The driver of the wrecker had to pass our house on his way back. When he saw that we had just arrived, he pulled in behind us so he could help Bob unload us from his van. My heart sang with gratitude. He did not have to do that, but what an added blessing. *May God return the kindness to him a hundredfold.*

This time the garage kept the van for two weeks and ended up running two tanks of gas through it as it sat in their bay, waiting for it to "mess up." It did mess up and they learned it was the fuel pump. Replacement! No more breakdowns.

I began making phone calls that night to get another vehicle because I knew God was speaking to my heart as I had asked Him to do that very morning.

CHAPTER SIXTEEN

UP, UP, AND AWAY, MAYBE

"*H*ello? Can someone help me schedule my husband for physical therapy?" I queried. "He's been in the hospital for a week with a blood clot in his hip. It has been ordered by the doctor."

The therapist was off that day.

"May I leave a message?"

Three days later when I had not yet heard from her, I called again and learned that she was on vacation. The next week when I finally reached the therapist, she came. She was austere, non-smiling, and matter-of-fact. She assessed the situation and refused to return until we had acquired a Hoyer lift. I learned it was a monstrous contraption to hook Al into to move him from the bed to the wheelchair, then to the bathroom and other locations inside our home. But she said another person at the company had to do the paperwork.

Upon reaching that person at the end of two weeks, I was told she was not the one who could help me. I would first have to have Mr. So-and-So authorize the order and get a prescription from the doctor, send the paperwork, have it approved by Medicare, etc., ad nauseam.

"We've never received that," was the routine answer when I called repeatedly to check on the necessary paperwork, even though the fax showed "message received." Who am I to say they had received it? What was the solution to this?

Did I need to call Medicare to verify that I was following the correct procedure? Weeks were passing and Al still had not had an evaluation, much less the therapy he so desperately needed. Medicare was unable to verify anything, and I got as many different answers as the number of phone calls I made. I called some of the numbers so often that I memorized the Muzak.

Al had to have another appointment with the doctor to be evaluated and then submit the forms to Medicare for approval. No communication transpired for weeks. When I contacted the company ordering the lift, the person handling our case was at lunch.

"When may I call back to reach her?"

"Oh, she'll be back in an hour."

So I called back, adding a few minutes' leeway in case she had a big lunch. When I reached her office, the person who answered said, "Oh, she's on leave this week."

Does lightning strike twice in the same place? Keep plowing ahead, my dear!

I asked with whom I could speak regarding the status of our lift. It turned out "she" was not even the correct person, even though I had been told to call her. They gave me the name of a guy who would make the decision, but he wasn't in. Frustration and disappointment reigned.

Meanwhile, Al had to sit day after day without the help he needed while they played games with me. Therapy was so very critical, but all had to be put on hold while phone messages, paperwork, Medicare, and computers (which were always "down" and became the scapegoat when personnel couldn't produce) fouled up and got blamed for the holdup.

"He" finally contacted me and said, "You'll have to get your doctor to evaluate Al and order the lift."

No amount of stomping, screaming, groaning, or moaning did any good. Weeks had gone by! Inside, I was saying, *"Hey, fellow, your village called and they're missing their idiot!"*

I just took a deep breath and, after making sure they indeed didn't have the paperwork, started again from the beginning. Following many weeks of all this nonsense, the company finally called and said the lift was in. *Be still, my heart.* After months of chasing the wind and getting the run-around, the monstrous thing was ready to be delivered, the instrument that was to be the gateway to vast opportunities of therapy and giving Al what he needed to get better.

Delivery day dawned. The miracle lift barely went through the front door of the house. The next hurdle was the bedroom door. By taking off a strip of molding, we finally got it into the bedroom. You'll never guess! The legs of this albatross wouldn't fit under the bed—an absolute necessity for getting it close enough to the bed to pick up Al. At that moment, I felt as if I had spent all my life's savings to go to Rome, and when I got there the pope was on vacation.

Some dear friends learned of the problem and immediately cut some two-by-four blocks that fit under the legs of the bed to raise it enough to accommodate the lift. And they didn't just make the blocks, they came and lifted the bed and put the blocks in place. I was so grateful!

The next day, reporting the so-called victory to Home Health brought no excitement. We learned it would be another week before the therapist could come out and demonstrate the lift.

The same stone-faced therapist arrived and immediately took charge. She whipped out the "sling" made of what looked like a strong fishnet. She rolled Al over onto his side and positioned the net under his body, then rolled him back. I stood at the foot of the bed, observing closely. I knew this would soon become my responsibility.

She then positioned the arm of the lift above the bed and began to hook up the various rings on the edges of the net to the clips, for want of a better word, on the lift. I must say that in my observation I gradually became aware that the outcome was not going to be as she thought. I was thinking, *I wonder what is really going to happen when she cranks this thing up,* but I wouldn't touch that with a ten-foot pole! I stood still at my station and watched intently, silently. When she finished, she proudly announced that she would then show me how easy it was to transfer Al without hurting the caregiver's back.

The moment of truth had arrived. I held my breath. She took hold of the handle to crank up the lift, and when she did Al's feet went up in the air and his head went down! It was all I could do to keep my composure. I stifled a giggle, kept a poker face, and said, "So *that's* how it's done."

She would not make eye contact with me. She hid her embarrassment by saying the new models were different from the ones to which she was accustomed. But, never having seen one, even I knew she was connecting it incorrectly.

We completed more paperwork that day to finish the deal. But she didn't suggest another visit, even though I understood from the doctor that she was to come two or three times a week for about six weeks. Still no therapy was done; instead she gathered her things and left. We had the major item for therapy now, so why wasn't it being used? The contraption took up space in our bedroom for six or seven months until I couldn't stand to look at it anymore. I asked a friend who had a large shed on her property if she could give it a home there, and she agreed. We disassembled it, loaded it in her jeep, and took it for a ride. Unloading it at the site where it would reside, she retrieved a quilt and threw it across the top. We put our hands over our hearts, recited some sentimental parting words, walked out, and locked the door. It remains there to this day.

After all this nightmare and months of headaches, poor Al never received therapy because the therapist never came back. She was never in when I called to inquire. Maybe she was too embarrassed to show up.

Lord, what would You have me learn from this? Is this a lesson in perseverance? How could I have handled this whole thing better so that we would have reached our goal for Al's sake? Help me deal with the hurt and disappointment for Al. He is the one who has suffered because we were never able to achieve success through it all.

CHAPTER SEVENTEEN

NIGHTMARE DENTAL CARE

"*C*an your dental office accommodate a wheelchair patient?"

"Oh sure, no problem."

Well, that's good; at least we won't have to pay a specialist for cleaning.

Al had suffered from periodontal disease in the last twenty years and needed more than a standard cleaning. Having been ill for quite some time, other things took priority and for over two years he had not received proper dental care. Sometimes weather-related circumstances caused cancellations, sometimes we put his care on hold for other reasons, and sometimes he simply didn't feel up to it. Whenever I called to reschedule the appointment, it would take several weeks before they had an opening.

Upon our arrival and completion of the necessary paperwork, the hygienist came to the waiting room door and yelled, in what I as a former schoolteacher would call her "outdoor voice," "MR. MIMBS!" She certainly left no question as to who was being called. I stood up to wheel him back to the examining and X-ray room. As I followed, she continued to shout questions and commands at him, and I, being the sweet, kind person that I am, smiled and whispered, "He's in a wheelchair, but he isn't deaf!"

She turned to look at me, shrugged her shoulders, and said, "Well, you never know. . ."

When it came time for the cleaning, Al needed to be transferred. I asked the hygienist if she would please stand on the other side of the dental chair while I moved Al from the wheelchair to their chair. I explained, "Just in case I get overbalanced as I'm trying to dodge the overhead light, the tray table, and the equipment."

"No," she replied, "I can't do that–I have a bad back."

It took me a moment to process that statement.

Then I inquired if anyone else of the other dozen or more personnel in the office could lend me some assistance. "No," she stated, "they all have bad backs too."

I made a mental note to have my orthopedic doctor contact this office–he could make a killin'!

But now what? After calming myself, I prayed a desperate prayer, assessed all the obstacles and their locations, inhaled deeply, and carefully hoisted Al over to the dental chair. Success!

When the hygienist was ready to begin, she asked me if I would hold Al's head still while she went to work on his teeth. Now remember that I am a nice person, and because of that I never have an impure thought. My mind raced. Oh boy! Here's my opportunity! But I thank God I "kept a watch over the door of my lips," as the psalmist said (Psalm 141:3b), and only *thought* of saying, "Sorry, but I have a bad back."

The remainder of the visit offered more of the same. I observed as she loudly chatted away that she handled all the tools and placed them on the tray, *then* put on her gloves. She continued to talk to both of us as if our Beltones had faulty batteries. Other hygienists and dentists alike leaned out the doors of the adjacent offices to see what on earth was going on.

When it was all over, imagine my surprise when I went

up to the desk to check out and realized the charges had been doubled! I did not question. I scribbled the check, avoiding eye contact with anyone who may want to ask me if I wanted to schedule a follow-up visit, put the wheelchair in high gear, and fled to the van, taking the corners on two wheels, thankful that somehow we survived this humiliating experience.

Immediately, we began to look for another dentist. Thank God, we found a wonderful dentist who I think is the most compassionate, competent, patient, skilled man in all of Tennessee. What a blessing to discover this dental office relatively close to our house with a staff trained in accommodating handicap patients. He and his entire staff knew how to speak to us in normal tones. Whenever I had my cleaning and Al was in the waiting room, the dentist would go out to check on him and bring me a status report, assuring me that he was all right.

Thank You, Lord, for providing once again.

CHAPTER EIGHTEEN

WHEELCHAIR THEFT

Who, may I ask, would steal a wheelchair?

Several years after the onset of Al's illness and before his condition became severe, we took a plane trip out West to visit his sister and her husband. What a wonderful time of sightseeing and getting together with family and old friends! Restaurant and hotel staffs were very accommodating and assisted us in various ways. Airline personnel gave individual attention as needed. When we arrived back in St. Louis and got ready to disembark, we were unable to find Al's wheelchair. It was tagged with our ID, but apparently someone had decided to "borrow" it for their personal use.

The airport had one available, but that was not the issue. Airport personnel said we could borrow theirs until they were able to locate our chair, and we could use it to transport Al from the terminal into the car, but their chair would not fold for us to take it with us. Eventually we had to get Al out of the car, into the house where my sister-in-law lived, and later home to Tennessee.

I was instructed to go to the claims office. They would initiate a search and also work on getting a replacement. Well, the replacement was to be taken with us until they found ours. Then they would come to our residence and exchange the two wheelchairs.

Remember, their chair could not be folded and put into our car. What were we to do when we got home? How would Al get from the car into the house? What if they didn't find our chair?

In frustration, I paced at the counter while the lone attendant answered the phone and waited on other passengers. With each phone call that came in, I expected to receive news that the chair had been located. No such call came. Finally he said "Just a moment" before he went into the back room.

Several long minutes later another attendant came to the counter and asked if she could help me. I said I was being helped by a young man. She told me that the other attendant HAD GONE TO LUNCH! We had to start all over. Exhausted after the long wait following our five-hour flight, we had to go to Plan B.

My sister-in-law's friend who had come to the airport to pick us up remembered she had her deceased uncle's old wheelchair in her basement and offered us the use of it. We were able to get Al into the car using the airport's wheelchair, drive to the home of our driver-friend to pick up her uncle's wheelchair, and finally get to my sister-in-law's house to spend the night.

The next day about noon we received the call from the airline that our wheelchair had been located, and it would be delivered within about an hour. What a relief!

Lord, please watch over our belongings. Take care of us when we travel. You know we need a wheelchair. Thanks for loving us and working out a solution even while we are frustrated.

Lesson: Put a gigantic sign on your wheelchair that cannot be removed: THIS IS A STOLEN WHEELCHAIR!

CHAPTER NINETEEN

PLEASE HELP!

*T*he feeling one gets from sitting in a wheelchair reminds me of when I was a kid and we had swings made by tying a rubber tire to the end of a rope and hanging it from a tree limb. After swinging for awhile, our hipbones felt bruised and our bottoms and legs went numb. Try *living* in this position. Standard wheelchairs are killers for comfort and posture. The "sling" effect of the seat puts pressure on the sides of the buttocks, causing an uncomfortable and unnatural side-to-side curve.

The back of the chair is at a 90-degree angle and pushes the upper body forward, squeezing the stomach, heart, and lungs unnaturally. The occupant's head and shoulders sag while their feet and legs hang down. In Al's case, he had to keep this position for roughly fourteen hours a day. My heart ached as I watched him deteriorate further and further.

Within a few short hours he would begin to moan. When I asked what the problem was, he would declare, "I hurt."

"Where do you hurt, darling?"

"My butt."

Poor Al, as he rode in his wheelchair, was at the mercy of a number of well-meaning people. Lots of obstacles presented themselves in the day-to-day routine. For the most part those who saw us approaching a door would jump up and run ahead of us to open it, offering any kind of help they could. I had begun lately to say, "Please thank your mother for teaching you good manners." This usually evoked interesting responses that ranged from "Yes she did and I will tell her" to "Well, Mama's gone and Daddy died last year, but they did try to teach me right."

I've observed sometimes at the doctor's office still others who may be reading and peek from behind their book to get some free entertainment. *How will they negotiate the obstacles to get inside? Will she back in or go in forward? Can she prop the door open with one foot, grab the handle with the left hand, depress the back of the chair with her right foot to get the front wheels over the threshold, lean against the self-closing door with her shoulder, and try not to develop a hernia as she is pushing with all her might?* Meanwhile, the onlooker is amused by my antics as we struggle to just get Al through the door. Duh!

I launched a campaign for a chair that would tilt back, have a flat seat, and a cushion with air "fingers" to permit better blood flow. Foot rests should be designed so they could be raised. An ideal chair would allow various positions to alternate the pressure points. This chair was not to be a luxury but rather a necessity.

The search began and along with it negative responses. "You are not eligible because you, through Medicare, purchased a power chair."

Medicare, before their guidelines changed, readily approved power chairs left and right at $5,000 a pop. Salesmen and manufacturers profited greatly. It didn't work for Al, but he had one anyway. When the representative came to the house to demonstrate the chair, I was very straightforward. I explained in detail that it would not work for him. Period. Instead, they left the chair, stating that he would "get used to it." Having the power chair now disqualified him for something that *would* help him. He could not get another chair until five years had passed.

Because of his neurologic impairment, Al could not transfer information from his brain to his hands to operate the chair. Once he accidentally moved the stick, left tire tracks on my foot, ran into a decorative ceramic statue, and smashed it beyond repair. Crying and hopping on one foot, I pulled his driver's license right then!

Persistently, I inquired how we could get the desired piece of equipment. Just as persistently, I was refused. This company, that company... All the while Al was becoming more and more uncomfortable, more and more bent forward, his head resting on his chest with the muscles in the back of his neck lengthening and the muscles in front becoming shorter. Therapy was recommended, but without a change in his daylong position it produced minimal results.

Persistence produced this lead and that lead, another wild goose chase, and yet another dead end until finally we thought there was no other avenue. Then one day, miraculously, we found a company—an hour's drive away—that agreed to measure Al and work with us to get the coveted chair, but once again when we started the proceedings, we met with failure.

I refused to give up. There had to be a way. Upon their denial, and after much questioning and pleading and, yes, whining on my part, they vaguely recalled the name of a company in a nearby larger city that might be able to help us. It was always worth a try. I would continue to grasp at straws!

We made and kept the appointment. Hours and hours were spent getting this approved and that approved, ad infinitum. A full-blown circus! Al made me very proud. He was so patient and cooperative. I began to hope that this wheelchair might actually become a reality. It could be that Al sensed it too.

He was measured again. This time all the requests and

requirements gradually fell into place. They measured every-thing—the distance between his third toe and his thumb, and from his eyebrows to his bellybutton. He was worn out by the time they got all the paperwork finished.

It would take another six to eight weeks to get the chair, but meanwhile they had a Roho cushion in stock with the coveted air fingers. The cost? Four hundred dollars, plus tax, up front. But God had gone before us. Through a refund we had recently received unexpectedly, we had the money to get the cushion that very day! I could read it on Al's face; he enjoyed immediate relief as his body was lowered onto his old chair, but with the comfort of the new cushion.

Thirteen months passed from the time I started the search until we actually possessed the chair. Unfortunately, it was too late for his overall posture and he now had to sit with his chin on his chest most of the time. But at least the pain from sitting in the "sling" was alleviated. The tilt allowed the angle of the chair to be changed as often as necessary to change the pressure points.

Talk about the pain of birthing an elephant! I can testify it was worth it.

CHAPTER TWENTY

WHAT IS IT?

"What is that? I've never seen anything like it."
During Al's bed baths I noticed that he was developing a reddish, slightly raised spot about the size of a half dollar on his lower back just above the end of the spine. It wasn't a sore, but I knew something was wrong that needed attention. Almost overnight it developed into a leathery-looking dark scab with an even larger raised area that would take my entire hand to cover.

We made an appointment with the doctor, who just leaned Al forward in his wheelchair, took a two-second look at the spot, declared it a "decubitus," and ordered a Home Health wound care specialist. He said I needed a prescription for a cream that would "eat the dead tissue," and if I got any of it on the good tissue it would eat that too.

Fear struck my heart. *What if I do something harmful? What if this stuff is dangerous? Why is this on the market for non-professionals to use?* So I went to the pharmacy and engaged the expertise of my trusty pharmacist friend, who researched the chemical ingredients and assured me that it would not be dangerous to use if I followed the instructions.

Several days later, when the Home Health nurse came to treat this thing, I gave her my own assessment, calling it a "mound of infection" under that bulge.

"Oh, no," she declared confidently, examining the hot, red bulge, "that's just fluid."

My gut feeling ran contrary to the medical diagnosis. *What shall I do? Just sit here? What is happening to the tissue under this scab?* I had plenty of time to think about it. Another week went by before someone came to treat it. I was distressed because of what I envisioned happening inside the wound. Time was of the essence.

When the wound care specialist came she carefully covered the dark leathery spot with the tissue-eating salve and topped it with a bandage. Inside my brain, I protested wildly. *What good will that do against the hard scab that has developed?*

Two days went by and nothing changed. On her return visit, she took a scalpel and cut a grid on the scab to allow the salve to penetrate. More time went by. I have to tell you that with each bath time, my anxiety increased. Having no previous experience with this, was I justified in my concern? Should I bypass all the medical advice and find a specialist? What was this going to do to Al? It had now been four weeks since I first noticed it. The mound got to be the size of the palm of my hand, more pronounced, shiny red, and, in my estimation, full of infection.

More salve, more bandages, more time went by, and on a Saturday Al began vomiting, had a fever of 102, a heart rate of 137, and was very ill. I believed the infection had spread throughout his body.

It wasn't even a toss-up. I rushed him to the emergency room. After six hours of observation, they admitted him. I pointed out the decubitus, but they said that wouldn't have anything to do with what was going on. My feeling was very strong that it *did*.

When the primary care doctor came in the next day, I again addressed the infection and showed him how it had progressed.

"Well, that wouldn't have anything to do with this."

How can you say that? No further treatment was done on the decubitus.

I kept very close tabs on it because it had grown and had a fiery red appearance. And Al was so very sick!

On Tuesday, it broke open and at least six to eight ounces of infection drained onto the bed.

I had restrained myself to the limit. How could this be happening in a hospital with medical professionals who were familiar with this kind of thing? I pitched a fit, and *this* time, in anger, I added, "You will do something about this today!"

"Well," the doctor said hesitantly, "I have contacted Dr. So-and-So. Hopefully, he will be able to check it for us."

With my finger pointing at his chest, I said, "TODAY! YOU WILL DO SOMETHING TODAY!"

By 4 p.m. that day, Al was in surgery with general anesthesia to clean out this so-called "fluid."

The next day when it was time to change the bandage I saw the Stage Four hole on Al's backside, large enough to hide a ping pong ball. Two tunnels more than two inches long extended from the hole. The bone was visible! I almost passed out. *This* was a bedsore? *Why, why, why? Why wasn't something done weeks ago? Why was it allowed to escalate to that magnitude before something was done?* I vowed that it would NEVER happen again.

I cried tears of repentance, tears of regret, tears of sorrow that I had not done more to get treatment sooner. *I failed you, Al. I am so sorry! Please forgive me! Lord, please help me to forgive those who I feel wronged us by not listening, doing something, and explaining what was going on. Help me!*

The twice daily cleansing, packing, and dressing was almost overwhelming. The surgeon came in and walked me through the steps and techniques he wanted to be used in caring for the wound. Since I never left Al's hospital room, I witnessed this procedure numerous times, asking questions and absorbing all the information. It was very intimidating at first, but watching the procedure repeatedly made it easier. Of course, I was not allowed to participate in the dressing of the wound except to hold Al's body in position so they could do their job, but I assumed that one day when I took him home, I would have to be responsible for his care.

The surgeon turned the wound care over to the hospital's physical therapists, who came to the room on a regular basis to perform twice daily treatments on the wound. We had met this nice, young therapist two years earlier when he evaluated Al in the hospital for physical therapy. He carried on a friendly conversation, including things going on in his personal life. He seemed to have rapport with us.

But during Al's wound care, when I felt the "expert" was not performing the task as the doctor had demonstrated, I questioned the therapist, stating that the surgeon said to do it *this* way. In my effort to help Al get the best care for this horrible wound, did I do the wrong thing? Apparently, I did.

The fight was on! An RN who was assisting observed the whole thing. The physical therapist whirled around to face me and through gritted teeth said, "I am the professional here. I'm trained to do this and I know what I am doing." Closed conversation. I retreated into silence as he spent the remainder of the time completing the task.

He gathered his supplies, pulled off his gloves, and left the room. The nurse followed him out while I sat down to ponder what had just happened. *Is there more than one way to skin a cat? Did I overstep my bounds? Did I show a lack of trust? Was it an ego issue?* Within a few minutes the same nurse bolted back into the room and with great concern in her voice inquired, "Are you all right?"

"Yes," I answered calmly, "why do you ask?"

"I am so sorry. He never should have spoken to you that way! I am so sorry."

I smiled. "If that's the worst thing that ever happens to

me, I'll be a blessed person. It's okay, and maybe I had it coming."

"No, no! I really reprimanded him and told him it better not happen again." I thanked her and pondered a bit more about forgiveness. *Lord, HELP!*

Al was in the hospital for nineteen days with twice daily treatment for the bedsore, double pneumonia, MRSA, and C-diff, which requires nurses and visitors to don mask, gloves, and gown before entering the room. More vomiting, subsequent checking for a blockage, allergic reaction to the "cocktail" he had to swallow for the test, resulting in wild diarrhea that lasted for more than fourteen hours and caused a severe rash every place the fluid touched.

In came the nurses to put their standard cream on him after cleaning him, changing the bed, and changing him. I recognized the tube at once as a cream that had been used before and to which he was highly allergic. I asked her not to use it.

Whew! That was a close one. I was glad I caught it just in time. Ha! Instead, the nurse squeezed out a big glob of the cream and proceeded to rub it on his bottom, saying, "Oh, we use this all the time; it's good." *What am I, chopped liver? Am I stupid? What did I just say? LISTEN TO ME!*

As soon as she left the room, I drew a bath pan of water, used his soap I brought from home, and washed off the cream.

Two other nurses came into the room to confirm that the cream the offending nurse put on Al really was a good cream. I stepped up to the circle of nurses and told them I had ordered another over-the-counter brand cream that we used at home which I knew would not cause a reaction. They informed me that it was "not on the list" and therefore they could not get that brand.

I needed a Valium lick. My anger rose as adrenalin coursed through my veins. Keeping my voice even, I said,

"Well, we can fix that! I will go right now to the drugstore down the street and get a tube."

"Oh, no, no," they all protested in concert. "You can't bring in medicine from outside." To which I replied, "You just watch me."

I actually forgot momentarily Whom I represented. I parted the group of nurses, marched past them, stomped to the door, and headed down to the elevators. Off I went. I purchased the cream from the drugstore, returned to Al's room, and put it on him myself. Of course, we first had to stop the medications causing the allergy before we could start on the raw flesh caused from the horrible diarrhea.

As I was applying this cream, I calmed down. Then I discovered Al had developed a rash that covered his chest and abdominal area, a new reaction to a new intravenous antibiotic. When I called it to the attention of the nursing staff, they said they would have seen it eventually; the reason they didn't find it earlier was because I had interfered.

Words wouldn't come. God was probably protecting me from committing murder! *Lord, I know there's something I'm supposed to be learning here, but right now I'm not even thinking clearly. I am so focused on Al's suffering, and my heart seems to be closed to Your voice.*

Awake nearly all night, I had an option to watch television. I could learn everything I always wanted to know about the heartbreak of toenail fungus, or root for my team on *Cupcake Wars*. Decisions, decisions. In the nineteen days that Al was in the hospital, I left him a total of an hour and a half. During that window of time I wondered, *What can they do to harm him while I'm gone?* We lived a short distance away; I could drive home, grab the mail, throw some clean clothes into a bag, and head back to the hospital almost before they knew I was gone. During my 24/7 vigil, I learned a lot.

An RN prepared to give Al a bath by putting about ten

washcloths *into the sink* and turning on the hot water while she gathered the other necessary items. I watched carefully, wondering how she was going to proceed. When the water became hot enough to suit her, she squeezed out a washcloth to begin bathing Al.

Horrified, I stopped her. "Do you have any idea what I have observed as I've sat in this room all day and all night? Are you aware of all the stuff that has been put into that sink? And even if only hand-washing took place, that in itself would deem the sink dirty. Please don't put those washcloths on Al's body. Isn't there a bath pan to use?"

"Oh, it's okay, we do it all the time," she said.

"Well, this time I don't think so," I said. "Please allow me to take care of his bath." I retrieved the bath pan, got the necessary clean linens, and gave him a total bath myself. *Lord, do I have an anger buildup? Am I riding a broom? Am I unreasonable? What are You working within me? I simply can't let these things just drop. Al's comfort and health are involved. Please, help me!*

Other things were difficult as well. I decided it was time to confer with the CEO of this new, expensively furnished hospital. I requested an appointment and he came to our room. He was a bit reserved and seated himself stiffly in the chair opposite me. I had a list ready. Now, mind you, I can be professional when I have to.

I asked him if he was aware that the nurses had to run the water a long time before it got hot enough to use for a bath. The same was true in the shower. I pointed out that it was money going down the drain. He admitted he was not aware.

I also inquired if an additional chair could be brought into our room. If more than one person at a time visited, someone had to stand or sit on the bed. "No," he said with a smile, "because it will scratch the floor to move the chairs around." Priorities? In recording all visits and phone calls to Al's room during that period of 19 days, I counted 87 visits, more than 120 phone calls, and dozens of get-well cards.

There was also no place for hanging clothes, either the patient's clothing or a caregiver's. No hook in the bathroom for a robe or towel. "That's because this is a disability room," he explained. *I'm sorry, but that doesn't compute.*

Then I addressed another situation. One day during our stay, a disturbing emotional commotion took place down the hall. A large family was sobbing, talking loudly, wailing, and screaming. I looked out to see if I could determine what was wrong and made my way to the sitting area where the elevators came up. I quietly asked one family member if I could help. She sobbed, "No, God, please don't take my granny– you can't take my granny, I need my granny!" I put my arm across her shoulders. She said her granny had just coded, but they were able to resuscitate her and were moving her to a larger hospital.

I prayed with the grieving granddaughter and comforted her. All the while, visitors who got off the elevator on that floor stopped and stared. *Why didn't the staff nearby direct this grieving family to the hospital's "comfort" room?*

I had been in it once for coffee, so I located the room, tried the door, but it was locked. No one came to their assistance. The nurses just bustled about as usual, never making eye contact, leaving this family to their distressed emotional state in public view.

When I described this situation to the CEO he said, "Oh, yes, someone should have taken them."

I told him the door was locked. Why?

"Well, we do have to keep it private." I suppose it was a museum, not a place to be utilized. Sigh!

The movie *Bridge on the River Kwai* came to mind. Was it William Holden who lost his perspective?

My further comments included suggestions for ways to fix the problems I had encountered. I also told him I planned to follow up at a later time. My purpose was not to criticize but to offer solutions. Most were rejected, even to placing a hook on the inside of the bathroom door. He had some excuse for not doing it. One thing, however, was accomplished and that was fixing the hot water. Am I presumptuous to assume it was because this was the only thing that involved budgetary concerns?

A serious mistake happened the day the hospital discharged Al. I was given all the prescriptions to take by the pharmacy to have filled on the way home. Upon arriving home, I prepared the new daily regimen of medication, taking into account the directions on each bottle.

But wait! Something must be wrong. Before the day was over, I noticed he was not urinating enough. I checked all the bottles. There was no diuretic among them! This was a critical medication because he was diagnosed with congestive heart failure from excess fluid. I called the pharmacy asking them to check the prescriptions in case they had missed it. There was no diuretic listed. They offered to call the doctor to cover the diuretic.

What would have happened if I had not been vigilant? What about people who don't know what to expect certain medications to do? What about people who don't see well, or people who can't read or who don't understand?

Lord, please help me to always be alert to avoid costly mistakes, for Al's sake.

CHAPTER TWENTY-ONE

GUIDELINES MEAN
STOP SIGNS

*B*oth the general practitioner and the surgeon ordered that Al must have an air mattress. Tiny holes in the mattress allowed air forced by a motor to come through the sheet to keep Al's body dry and comfortable. Medicare approved this mattress and it was in place when Al arrived home. The doctors emphasized that he would have to be on one the rest of his life.

He also had a Home Health wound care nurse who came each day to dress the decubitus. When she arrived I asked her if she would mind if I changed the dressing under her supervision. She agreed, and when I finished she stated that she could not have done better herself. So daily for many weeks, when she came, I changed the dressing while she watched. She then took his vitals, recorded everything, and left. At bedtime, I repeated the procedure.

Five months later we were able to stop treating the decubitus. The two tunnels had finally healed and the Home Health nurses were dismissed. That very day, Medicare called to say they were coming to pick up the mattress.

"NO!" I exploded. "Both doctors have ordered that he

must use this air mattress for the rest of his life to prevent further bed sores."

The Medicare representative stated in a mechanical way that it was not in Medicare's guidelines to provide a mattress once the Home Health nurses were discontinued. I asked if it would help if the doctors wrote letters stating that Al needed this mattress to prevent further life-threatening sores.

"Well, as I have told you," she repeated, "it is not in Medicare's guidelines. We will send our representative to pick up the mattress on Monday."

I begged her to give me three additional days and she reluctantly agreed. I needed time to work something out.

I was stunned. *What can I do? Who can I call?* When they brought the mattress I remembered thinking it appeared to be in a very used condition. The delivery rep told me they were all in the same shape.

"But it has been carefully sanitized even though it looks faded and worn," he said, trying to reassure me.

Light bulb moment! Maybe I could buy this one from Medicare in spite of its deplorable condition. I called the Medicare rep with my suggestion. She offered to check for me and put me on hold.

When she returned, she said, "Yes, it can be purchased at just slightly over $10,000. And you would make payments of only $375 a month. That price would not include any maintenance or repairs."

Well, of course! At that price, let's just go ahead and get two! My heart sank.

Plan B. "Is there a graveyard where these used mattresses go when they die and no longer qualify for first-quality equipment?" I asked hopefully.

"No," she answered, "we just simply continue to use them."

Plan C. "Do you have a social worker who could assist me in finding a mattress?"

She gave me a short list of numbers, adding, "I don't think you will find this helpful, but you are welcome to try." What an encourager.

I called seven places and spoke with people who were supposed to be able to help me. The last dear lady, I think she was Number 10, sympathized with me but said it was "impossible in this lifetime." *What am I going to do? They're coming Monday!*

No one, absolutely no one, could help me. My thoughts raced back to the awful decubitus, the infection, the MRSA, C-diff, the hospitalization, Al's pain and suffering, his acute traumas, all the strong and harsh medications. Could we possibly endure a repeat performance? Could we survive another siege? "Lord," I cried out, "this is an impossible situation! We need a miracle." He answered me with the passage in 1 Chronicles 20:15b: "The battle is not yours, but God's."

Is it possible for me to put it into Your hands? Am I able to trust You completely to supply this urgent need?

Following the last refusal, I was sharing my frustrations on the phone with a longtime North Carolina friend who had several years before helped care for a mentally challenged neighbor now deceased. Even though the woman was not bedfast, she had to use one of the airflow mattresses to prevent skin breakdown. My friend was eager to ask the girl's parents if they still had the mattress and if so would they be willing to sell it. *It's Your battle, Lord,* I reminded Him. After some deliberation, they agreed to let it go. Thank God!

The next hurdle was to get the coveted mattress to Tennessee. A six-hour drive didn't seem to be possible, so I contacted UPS shipping in a nearby town. After many phone calls, I arranged to have the mattress both packed and shipped to me. All the family had to do now was transport the item to the shipping store. So far so good.

Two days later when the huge package arrived, it was delivered by a female UPS driver with whom I had a very meaningful conversation about her faith in Christ. What a joy to be able to share the plan of salvation with her and tell her how God had provided for us.

She battled similar issues as we because her twenty-eight-year-old son was a severe diabetic as well as mentally challenged. She faced the same "brick wall syndrome" of trying to get help from the system. I thought of the scripture quoted in the opening of this book about going through things and being comforted by God so that when others experience the same things, we in turn can comfort them (2 Corinthians 1:3-4). She was encouraged that day during our brief encounter.

Lord, was this all in Your plan? Nothing happens by accident or coincidence. Thank You for once again orchestrating everything that will bring glory to You.

Together we wheeled the parcel into the house and I signed for it. A boxed mattress is huge. I wrestled it out of the box, dragged it into the bedroom, and hoisted it up on the bed because it had to rest on top of the queen-sized bed that Al and I shared.

After the air mattress was in place it was time for the moment of truth. Remember, it had not been used for at least three years. I held my breath and plugged it in. When I turned on the switch, suddenly the mattress gave a great whooshing sound. My heart sank. One entire section was flat! Now what? A malfunction? A hole? *What shall I do?* All night I wondered if I had done the right thing to pursue this in the manner I had chosen.

The next day when the Medicare rep came to pick up their mattress, I demonstrated the problem for him. This wonderful angel of a guy immediately located what turned out to be a three-inch hole where the seam had separated; he instructed me to simply apply some crazy glue. Then we pressed the seams together, the total of a fifteen-second job. It worked! And for the cost of less than a dollar we were in business. By the way, out of the goodness of his heart, the rep thoroughly checked over the entire mattress I had acquired and pronounced it a Rolls Royce compared to the one we had been using. Al had no more sores or breakdown of the skin.

However, the remaining eighteen inches of mattress on which I slept was another challenge, but the sacrifice was worth it for Al's sake. Picture this: if I placed my back against the side of his mattress, my knees extended a couple of inches beyond the edge of my side of the mattress. If I turned the other way and put my knees against his mattress, well, you can guess what was hanging over the side of the bed!

The packing and shipping cost $97, plus the purchase amount (which wasn't quite $10,000, $200 to be exact), and now we had our own mattress!

Thank You, God! You are my Jehovah Jireh, my Provider. Help me to remember that You are always in control and that "your Father knows your need before you ask Him" (Matthew 6:8b).

CHAPTER TWENTY-TWO

GIVE ME A BREAK

$\mathcal{R}$ espite > noun: a short period of rest or relief from something difficult or unpleasant.

I can only figure it was through God's grapevine that a caregiver program heard of Al's situation and sent someone to evaluate him for eligibility to receive outside help. By this time, a day's respite, or even a few hours', would be such a blessing. Finding someone to stay with him became increasingly difficult.

Now, we had many friends who were happy to sit with Al while I ran a few errands. However, it wasn't always easy. Let me describe some of the situations I encountered. First of all, everyone became an expert. "You should. . ." "You need to. . ." "I would do 'so-and-so." I listened and then I would say, "By the way, do you think you could come over Thursday from two to four while I go to the dentist? You don't have to do anything, just be here."

"Oh, no, I'm so sorry," they would say, "I have such-and-such commitment that day. Maybe some other time." But that time never came.

The caregiver program sounded really good. Unfortunately, there was a waiting list of nine months. But the time went by quickly and soon we were interviewed for respite care. Their company had numerous resources from which to choose, matching the caregiver with the client. Their evaluation follow-up was so helpful to me to make sure the "fit" was suitable for Al's care.

We were granted a certain number of hours per year, and as time went on we also became eligible for receiving some of Al's personal supplies.

The ones in charge were absolutely wonderful and ever so helpful to send a caregiver who was able to meet Al's specific needs. He had to be fed, receive periodic position changes in his tilt chair, and of course, they had to have the phone at their elbow to answer my many "checking in" calls. My mind was never far from home.

In addition to his care, the program included some light housekeeping, dusting, sweeping, and even ironing! How wonderful to come home to a neat house and a row of freshly ironed clothes.

That was true respite for me.

Anyone who has a total-care person understands how much expensive briefs can drain the household budget. The briefs also have to be just right for the individual. For example, one year a company we had been ordering supplies from dropped out of sight and we could no longer purchase the desired style that was best suited for Al.

The respite care individual in charge from the company spent many hours endeavoring to find another company whose products worked for Al. She was indefatigable. In the process, she had numerous samples sent to us to try. Many of them were total disasters. But she never gave up. It took months to find exactly the right style supplies. I will remain forever grateful to the understanding people who assisted us and worked with us to make life just a little bit easier, and who even seemed to enjoy being helpful.

God, may Your abundant blessings be upon them for the kindness they showed Al and me.

CHAPTER TWENTY-THREE

SAME SONG, SECOND VERSE

*O*n a Thursday in May, Al had been running a fever, had a spongy cough, congestion, and a poor appetite. A visit to the local GP revealed severe dehydration along with the other symptoms. The doctor gave us papers to admit him directly to the hospital, thus bypassing the emergency.

Strangely, as we drove to the hospital I felt God impressing upon me that this was a test. I spoke my feeling to Al and thanked God for warning me.

By 4 p.m., we were in a hospital room and fluid IVs were started. Preliminary paperwork was done, vitals taken and recorded: blood pressure 82/63, temperature 101.1, heart rate 143. Following an EKG a heart monitor was connected. Al's dinner arrived but he ate very little.

Around 10 p.m., Al began having difficulty breathing. He had to cough in order to draw in oxygen. One attendant attempted to measure Al's oxygen, trying the device on each finger, to no avail. He even tried to get a reading by putting the device on Al's ear. Nothing! Meanwhile, the heart monitor at the nurses' station indicated that he had gone into atrial fibrillation. In response to the monitor, several nurses came into the room. Assessing the situation, I strongly recommended that we call a doctor. "HE NEEDS TO SEE A DOCTOR!" I finally shouted. Al was obviously in great distress!

As all the nurses stood around, the ensuing conversation went something like this:

"I'm not authorized to . . ."

"If you're *in* the hospital, you can't go to ER . . . in other words, you can't cross over."

"We can't call just any doctor that's in the hospital; he has to be *your* doctor."

"The only way you can get . . ."

I stood there in disbelief. "What does one have to do, call 911 and ask the paramedics to come to Room 516 and help Al?"

Eventually someone did call Al's doctor. We waited for him to return the call. *Where is he?*

Why does he not return the call? Somebody, PLEASE!

The doctor finally called back and prescribed a plan of treatment. No hurrying was evident. I learned later that because Al's living will stated "Do Not Resuscitate" they felt there was no point in hurrying. Finally someone went to get oxygen. Al was placed on number six or seven level of oxygen which helped him calm down and breathe more easily. Fluid was running at 100 percent to hydrate him. Chest X-rays revealed pneumonia and bronchitis; intravenous antibiotics were started. Antibiotics always concern me because Al is allergic to anything with sulpha or penicillin, and as you might well know almost all antibiotics contain both.

They administered bags and bags of fluid. His body began to look like a water balloon. Getting his briefs changed was a challenge for me because his hips and legs were extremely swollen. When I expressed my concern, I was told it was normal and that he had to have the excessive fluid in order to hydrate him.

Each day was a challenge. Al still had all the symptoms he displayed when admitted. But to me he was worse because of the excess fluid. Touching his skin was almost eerie. Bathing him was difficult because it was hard to wash the puffs of swollen skin and still get into the creases. He didn't want to eat, but I tried to entice him with various things I knew he liked. I "slept" in a chair next to his bed and monitored every move he made.

Four days into Al's hospital stay, a nurse came into the room with a syringe and headed toward the IV. I stopped her and asked what the medication was she was giving him. She replied, "40 mg Lasix."

"No!" I protested. "What is going on? We give him tons of fluid, then we take it back out?" Here we go! What they call a "water pill" to reduce fluid necessitates taking potassium to replace what was lost in excessive urination. Up to this point we had at my request avoided using a Foley catheter. But with increased output, there was no way we could keep up with the amount produced as a result of the diuretic. What could we do now? Catheters can cause urinary tract infections and bladder infections, and the medications often throw the body out of balance. "Please let me talk to someone who can tell me what is going on," I said. It seemed useless because I could not get it to compute in my brain.

The RN on the hall finally convinced me that Al had to have the diuretic, but I asked her if we could do 20 mg instead of 40 mg until a catheter could be in place. She honored the request.

Within the first forty-eight hours in the hospital, Al developed a decubitus, a bed sore! He'd had one two years before, so I knew what we were dealing with. In admissions I had requested an airflow mattress because I knew what could happen when he didn't have one.

The answer was, "Well, we don't know if we have one available or if we can get one." In desperation, I offered to go home and get the one off our bed and bring it in for him. (Ha! Did I really think that would go over?) Their immediate response was, "Oh, no, we would have to have special wiring and we can't have anything brought in."

I went into alarm mode. Had I not experienced this before with Al? Did I not understand the gravity of the situation? Did not my experience tell me what would come next as a result of this type of sore? Did I not alert someone to the fact that on his backside something very serious was developing? I ask you, does a cat not have a tail?

The powers that be said nothing could be done to treat it until it broke open. Then the wound care specialist would come to take care of it. I'm not a rocket scientist, but this line of thinking again did not compute. *Lord, I told You and I also promised Al that as long as I am alive, I would never let this happen again. What can I do?*

"Will you please get someone to treat that sore now?" I begged. "I know what will happen if it is left untreated. The last one required five months to heal."

"Oh, really?" The preoccupied attendant finished her linen change and left the room without even checking it. I might as well have told her the dog threw up on the carpet. She would probably have been more concerned about that.

When the doctor came in, I implored him to do something. He said he would get the wound care people to come the next day. Meanwhile, the sore was inflamed, oozing, and growing.

The mattress was brought in within twenty-four hours, but as we already knew, it was too late.

The expert arrived, assessed the decubitus, and went to work. When he pulled out a Duraderm patch, I cringed because Al was allergic to the adhesive in most dressings as well as latex. Only paper tape could be used on him.

"Please don't use that! Is there anything else that can be used? He is allergic . . ."

He interrupted me. "Oh, we use this on everybody."

This is always the standard quote.

No matter what the circumstances my common sense told me that one does not apply a very sticky glue patch directly onto an open draining sore. I felt so helpless against these "professionals." How could I stop this? I could picture in my mind what would happen when the sticky patch was pulled off.

When the patch was changed the next day, sure enough Al's epidermis came off with the patch and left an inflamed rectangle imprinted on his backside. When I pointed this out, the reply was, "That's just from us pulling it off." It took me nine weeks to clear up the skin irritation. The same thing happened with the salve they used all over his bottom and groin area. It was the worst case of diaper rash you could ever imagine! I cleansed his body with water and his own mild soap I brought from home, then used a special medicated powder and packed it with absorbent material until it cleared up.

Inside I started screaming again. *Why does it have to go all the way to the bone before anything can be done? Why isn't it an emergency to stop the eating away of the good tissue? Lord, help me to gain control and be calm even in the midst of the storm. What was it You spoke to me on our way here? THIS IS A TEST.*

Five days following the oxygen and heart rate episode on the night Al was admitted, an echocardiogram was ordered. That afternoon when the results came in, the doctor called me out into the hall and told me I needed to call in the family. I told him we had no family within the immediate area. "What are you talking about? What is wrong?" I asked.

The doctor gave me some numbers that indicated the blood test results. "What are you saying?" I didn't understand. Al's echocardiogram showed that he'd had a serious myocardial infarction, congestive heart failure, and electrolyte abnormalities. Al's heart was working between 15 percent and 20 percent. His oxygen level and blood pressure were very low, and he had developed double pneumonia, MRSA, and klebsiella (pneumonia). These last two infections required isolation. Everyone entering the hospital room had to wear a mask, gloves, and a gown.

My mind was unable to absorb all this information. Some things I understand without explanation, but others are foreign. The bottom line: Al could die at any moment.

Because of the myocardial infarction, he was placed on a medication that further lowered his blood pressure and caused a higher heart rate. He became very lethargic, preferred not to eat, and slept a lot. I asked the doctor if he could give him a medication that was not "together." Couldn't he be given two separate medications to somehow bring the heart rate down and bring the blood pressure up instead of the reverse? The doctor said he *had* to be on this medication. Why? It seemed that he already had a high heart rate and low blood pressure because of the reduced function of the heart. But what do I know? Please put the cookies on the bottom shelf.

Al stayed an additional fourteen days. Fourteen days of anxiety, strong medications, and antibiotics, most of which had to be changed because of allergic reactions. During the fourteen days, I patiently attempted to "educate" the nurses, who for the most part were kind but again treated Al in cookie-cutter fashion. The philosophy was, "If it's good for the guy in the next room, it must be good for Al too." By doing this, it actually helped me to focus on something other than the gravity of Al's condition. I never left his side.

Day by day, hour by hour, shift by shift, they gradually learned that they can't treat all patients alike. I told them to be sensitive to the instructions from the family member nearest to the patient. The key word is LISTEN. I told them I didn't leave Al to go home because, frankly, I was afraid to leave. I learned that at first the nurses kidded (maybe it wasn't kidding) about drawing straws to see who would have to answer the call light to Al's room, because of me! But when they truly listened and began to understand my position, they actually enjoyed coming in and responded accordingly. They saw that I wasn't unreasonable in my requests. One even went so far as to say, "If I am ever in the hospital, I want Al's wife to take care of me. She knows how!"

Miraculously, Al began to improve. Yet his blood pressure continued to be low at 81/55 and his heart rate was still high at 108 per minute. The chest X-ray showed improvement on his pneumonia. After twenty-one days, he was discharged with medications.

Health care nurses and wound care nurses came seven days a week to treat the wound, cleaning and packing it each morning; I took care of it at night.

Yes, Lord, this certainly was a test. Only You can determine whether or not I passed it. But I failed Al in a broken promise. Forgive me, Al. Forgive me, Lord. Help me from this day forward to be more determined to keep my promises. Help me to know what to do.

CHAPTER TWENTY-FOUR

WILL THE EXPERT PLEASE STEP FORWARD?

I am reminded of the story I heard of two men who bought a truckload of watermelons for a dollar apiece. Taking them to the market, they sold them for a dollar apiece. After counting their money at the end of the day they pondered momentarily and concluded that if they were going to make any money, they needed to get a bigger truck.

Days and nights ran together as we wondered when this wound would heal. We followed the ongoing recommendations of the doctors and surgeons. A bed sore that developed after only two days in the hospital and got treated at home seven days a week, twice a day, cleaned by the surgeon at least four times, and was packed and bandaged twice a day for more than nine months still showed no improvement. In the course of treatment, questions remained unanswered. *Do we need to get a bigger truck?*

Suggestions ran short on my end because the sore Al had two years before healed after about five months. We were a long way past that timeframe with no end in sight. When the wound care nurse inquired about using a wound vac, the surgeon said Al was not a candidate. When I inquired about going to a wound center, the family doctor shook his head and said we would "get germs there." Other options included various things that were shot down as soon as they were suggested.

Again, the Home Health nurse who worked so closely with me decided to meet with the surgeon to try to persuade him to order a different treatment that included packing the wound with 65 percent saline-treated gauze. He asked her if she wanted him to get another nurse! She replied, "No! I thought maybe we should try a different treatment." He finally relented and agreed to allow her to try it.

So we began to use the new treatment, which required packing the wound only once a day instead of twice. After three weeks no apparent healing in the wound had taken place.

At our next appointment with the surgeon, he decided he would send us to a wound center. The one they contacted took our appointment then called us the next day and said the clinic was closing permanently at the end of the week. *Lord, how can this always happen to me? Am I so in need of fixing? How long do I have to go around this same mountain?*

I asked the person who called if she could suggest another wound center in any of the nearby towns. After consulting the surgeon, they were able to make an appointment at another center for the following week.

The appointment day brought pouring rain that somewhat dampened my spirits. Was this another waste of time? Another wild goose chase? After traveling through the driving rain into another time zone, I was relieved to discover the building had a canopy over the door so at least we didn't get soaking wet. Inside, I observed that the waiting room was empty. *The first rule in the book is if there are no customers, drive on! But where would we go?* So we signed in and two nurses took us to an examination room. I transferred Al to the exam table where they took off the dressing and pulled out the packing.

The nurse cleaned the wound, took a photo, swabbed it for a culture, and prepared the site for the doctor. He entered and shook my hand. I hesitated to take his hand because I had been treating myself for a cold. The doctor moved around to the other side of the exam table to get a look at the wound. He began to touch and press, at which time I—no longer intimidated by medical personnel—boldly questioned, "Aren't you going to put on gloves?"

"Oh, yes, yes, yes!"

I didn't say it aloud, but I wanted to say, "When?" Two years earlier I wouldn't have ventured to speak up in that way, but I was past that stage and had no reservations. Al's care was what mattered. Remember, we had already been told by the other doctor that we would get "germs" at a wound center.

Following the doctor's exam, he ordered filling the wound with honey. My immediate thought was, *Al, now I can call you Honey Buns!*

They asked about my reaction to the honey. I said, "Anything short of leeches and maggots, I can be agreeable." They explained that Al didn't have enough infection to feed maggots. Wow! Thank God for small favors.

You may think I'm kidding, but in fact in some rare cases they do use this primitive aforementioned technique.

The next step included applying two patches, one overlapping the other, which made me very nervous. As the nurse peeled off the backing, it looked exactly like the patch used in the hospital that caused him so much irritation to the skin. I gently stopped her, voiced my concern, and asked her to please not use that patch because of his previous allergic reaction to the adhesive.

"Oh," she replied quickly, "this isn't the same thing–and we have never had *anyone* be allergic to this."

Same song, second verse. Did you hear what I just said? Al is not everyone else! I asked again that she please not use the patch, but to no avail.

Then she pulled out some kind of tape to which I again

protested. Only paper tape can be used. As she peeled off the backing of the tape she exclaimed, "This is better than paper tape; in fact, it is just like paper tape."

Taking a deep breath, I calmly said, "This is just a little hint: you don't want me to ride my broom."

My mind was made up as I left there. If by bedtime I noticed any redness or rash starting, I would remove the patches and tape and load Al into the van, drive to the nearest facility where he could be treated, and notify the wound clinic when their office opened the next day.

The next day Home Health called and said they had orders from the wound center to put a wound vac on Al the same day. It works by reverse pressure. By three o'clock, a rep from the company delivered the wound vac, and while he was still demonstrating the vac and going over all the paperwork, the Home Health nurse arrived.

My mind was whirling. *Here we go again with more tape, more glue, more possibilities for Al to have a reaction.* By Monday we received a call that his culture was positive for MRSA. He needed a prescription for antibiotics, strong antibiotics! I recognized the names of them immediately as those to which Al was allergic. But I called the pharmacy to verify and see if they could give me the names of some antibiotics we had substituted in previous times.

The doctor suggested Al be taken to the hospital to have a picc line put in to administer intravenous antibiotics. A representative called to say that Medicare would not cover it, his secondary insurance would not cover it, and his drug card would not cover it. The total approximate cost was over two thousand dollars!

THAT was not doable.

At the same time, a special bed was ordered. The company explained that the bed was designed with "sand" in the mattress that circulates and eliminates all pressure. Wonderful! The representative declared it the best in the business for pressure wounds. Of course, that's just what we needed. I inquired if it would fit on top of our queen-sized bed as did the airflow mattress. So many negative elements outweighed the positive things; the airflow mattress became almost ineffective, even though we continued to use it.

"No, it is an entire bed, frame, mattress, and headboard," she explained.

"Well, am I supposed to sell my furniture to accommodate this thing? Then when I no longer need the bed, and it goes back, what will I do for furniture?"

The rep queried, "Can't you just move some furniture around?" The only thing I could think of was to put it out on the front porch and let Al sleep out there! *Your cynicism is showing again.*

Back to the antibiotics. Thanks to the pharmacist, we identified one that Al had used before with success. Problem solved? No, because Al developed diarrhea that lasted five days, had no appetite, and ran a low-grade fever. He woke up each morning with wet sheets, wet sleepwear, wet pillowcase, and wet hair. It seemed we had used all alternatives, so they said we must tough it out until he had completed the prescription.

My heart hurt for him. As I watched him suffer, I cried out, "Please! Forgive me, Lord!" I was the one who administered the pill which in turn made him sick. I was the one who could undo what had been set in motion. I could say NO! But could he make it without the medicine? It was as if I were saying, "Here, Al, take this and feel sick." My struggle inside had all questions and no answers. I'd come to the point where my tears were almost dried up. Only frustration remained.

In the background we had conflicting opinions on the wound vac. The wound care center said there should be no foam inside the wound. The Home Health nurse said the foam promoted healing.

Upon removal of the wide tape, a quarter-sized blister had formed and broke open as the tape was pulled off. *What did I say about the tape?* Now we had another wound to treat.

Another Home Health nurse had concern about the technique of the wound center and instructed me that if any white edges appeared, I should call her immediately. Saturday evening when I changed Al, I noticed white edges. My nurse friend who was visiting strongly suggested I call. The on-call nurse, who drove thirty miles to check the situation, declared it was all right and eased my fears. However, she also assured me I had done the right thing.

For three full days after the wound vac was in place, no drainage was visible in the canister. Had the vacuum malfunctioned? Had it been properly connected? When the Home Health nurse came the following day, Al's breathing was extremely labored, he still was not eating, he had diarrhea, he was running a low-grade fever, and his blood pressure was even lower than usual. The labored breathing seemed to be the greatest concern, and the nurse suggested we go to the emergency room. This resulted in an eight-day hospital stay.

After that hospitalization, we were directed to another wound center, one that had not yet encountered me in their repertoire. The team changed the wound vac, placing the hard end of the tube inside the wound instead of forming a foam track over to his hip. This placement prevented his sitting or lying on the right side and/or being turned onto his side at night. As soon as I discovered the problem, I had to remove it, completely reposition the tube, and redress the wound.

When I called them at seven o'clock the next morning to inquire why they had done what they did, they laughed and said it was the proper placement and they did all their wound care that way. Believe me, it was not funny to me. All it did was produce more pain and suffering for Al.

We were due back there in two days. When we arrived, and before any wound care was done, I requested an opportunity to talk with the team. I explained the situation and stated that unless we could get on the same page, we needed to terminate the relationship. The entire atmosphere changed. Their attitude was much more agreeable and their performance more professional. *Thank You, God, that I was able to keep my cool in an adverse situation. Help me to keep on forgiving and to guard my own attitude when things go wrong.*

As it turned out, Al was too ill to return for further treatment.

CHAPTER TWENTY-FIVE

CHANGING DOCTORS, IF THAT'S POSSIBLE

*A*fter much deliberation I decided to change doctors. Events leading up to this included doctor visits that were helter-skelter and follow-up blood work reports promised for Tuesday that reached us on Friday afternoon, relayed by a nurse who didn't give me an opportunity to ask questions. I discovered the doctor had no clue what Home Health was doing with Al. He had no communication with them regarding certain things he had ordered when Al was released from the hospital weeks before.

When I told the doctor that no therapy was being done, he said physical therapists were supposed to have come seven days a week. I told him they had evaluated Al and determined that he did not need therapy. He registered shock! But why had he not received a report from them, or if he did, why did he not read it? Was he supposed to follow up? Was I? Red flags were flying.

Two EKGs were done in the office. The battery went dead. Printouts were not working; we finally got results, but according to the doctor they were incorrect. My major concern was that he never looked at Al's second decubitus that developed after two days in the hospital. Remember, he had experienced a horrific sore less than two years before that took five months to heal.

The list went on. Should I confront? Should I discuss? I had endured all I could handle. *Help me forgive.*

I called the surgeon Al had in the hospital previously, but no appointments were available for five weeks. Could we be placed on the cancellation list? All the time the sore was growing, and I knew this time what it was and what could and would happen if it was not treated.

I called two doctors' offices, both doctors having been on call when Al was in the hospital. One was not taking any new patients, so my prayer for direction seemed to be answered. I made an appointment with the other one.

When I explained the circumstances, they worked us in the next day and set up an appointment for the following day with the surgeon, who previously said his office had no openings for the next five weeks.

This second decubitus had the same appearance as the first one two years earlier. Inflamed, swollen, with a leathery burgundy-colored center, located near the sacrum and slightly to the left, he now had matching sores. *Lord, please!*

With my help the surgeon positioned Al on the exam table, the height of which would give a normal person a nosebleed. I held Al in place while the doctor worked. He deadened the surrounding tissue by injection, took scissors, and clipped out the plug of the decubitus. Infection drained from it, so it had to be packed and dressed.

He suggested a new Home Health company; I told him it was his call. And what a change from the former company! Sometimes we don't know what we don't know. Don't be afraid to make changes just because you worry about what someone will think. Remember, most of the time it doesn't mean that a certain person or company is not reputable; it simply means that the relationship is not a good fit. We must do what is best for our loved one. You and I are responsible. And don't be afraid to make changes to bring improvement.

One week later we went back to the surgeon for further surgery, more anesthetic, more pain and swelling, more drainage, and now a deeper hole. The tissue was sent for analysis. Results showed staph infection! Now we had to have more strong antibiotics. Meanwhile, the tissue inside the sore took on a gray appearance. I suggested to the Home Health nurse that maybe we needed to use the cream that "eats the dead tissue." She called the surgeon and started the cream on Tuesday.

On Wednesday I was aghast when we turned him over to treat the wound. A hard lump the size of a marble had formed next to the sore being treated.

I exclaimed, "Oh no! Not another one!"

She felt the lump and pronounced it bone, nothing to be concerned about. "See? Feel it–it's just bone."

I said, "If it's bone, he grew it overnight. It was not there yesterday." *Lord, would You help me to know how to proceed? I have to do something!*

By that night when I changed the dressing, the lump had a white center, and by the next day the top of it had turned burgundy–exactly like all the others. More panic seized me. *Someone, please do something! What can I do? Lord, please help me–give me wisdom!*

The next day I waited and waited for the nurse to show up. When I called they explained some mix-up had occurred–blah, blah, blah. She just couldn't make it. Plan B. Since I had been doing all the wound care previously, I just followed the treatment rules, cleaned it, packed it, and bandaged it myself. In calculating the schedule, I decided it would not be risky since we had a doctor's appointment on Friday afternoon.

When the new GP looked at the wound sight by leaning Al forward in the wheelchair, the entire new area had swollen and taken on the appearance of a decubitus except it had not yet broken open. The doctor gave orders for two strong antibiotics and two vitamins, and since our appointment with the surgeon was not until Monday, he asked us to go by the hospital for X-rays of the lower spine to see if osteomyletis, or inflammation of the bone, had set in.

The doctor explained again and again that the sore came from pressure that stopped the blood flow. I knew that. If I turned him on his left side he got a red spot on his left hip and left shoulder. If I turned him on his right side the same thing happened on the right hip and shoulder. *I need YOU to tell me what to DO about it!* My gut feeling–my opinion–was that he absolutely did not know.

Because Al had allergic reactions to many medications, I asked the pharmacist if we could get just two pills of each prescription. If it turned out that Al couldn't take the drug, we would not have to pay the price of a full prescription. The one particular antibiotic was extremely powerful and, as the doctor had explained, could not be taken with dairy products.

This was going to be tough. We relied a lot on cottage cheese and fruit, cheddar cheese on toast, milk on cereal, and of course ice cream. I questioned how long this restriction would need to be followed. Noting my worried tone, he added that if we kept two hours between the pill and the dairy product, it would be all right.

When I went to pick up the prescription, it had a hand-written sticker on the bottle that read "Take with milk." Not again! I felt like screaming. Whom could I trust? I called the pharmacy to inquire and found that it was a mistake.

At our next doctor's visit, I whined to him that I was so weary of having to be the doctor, watchdog, guardian, and whatever else. I had to watch everything like a hawk. He said maybe I was too *intense*. Red flag!

I bristled. "Listen, Doctor, you have a mundane, generic doctor/patient relationship, but I have a totally devoted love relationship, a lifetime investment, a one-flesh relationship of almost fifty years. But of course you wouldn't understand that would you?" I left there with a broken heart.

On Monday we had an appointment to see the surgeon. He was rather surprised and disappointed to see the way the decubitus had deteriorated rather than improved. A gray mass filled the area that had been debrided two weeks before. Upon removal of the gray dead tissue, it revealed a tunnel with liquid infection. My insides wept. *Here we go again. Who will deliver us from this awful plague? God! Al! Forgive me!*

Less than a week later, Al's heart rate was irregular and his oxygen level was low. Should I call the doctor? The surgeon was out of town, but we made an appointment with the GP. I was determined that the doctor would *see* the wound inside this time instead of simply leaning Al forward in the wheelchair and checking the outside flesh.

We waited an hour past our appointment time. At times we waited so long I memorized all the magazines in the waiting room. However, I had learned to check at the reception desk after twenty minutes to find out if there was a problem and if we should reschedule. Don't be afraid to do that. I admonish everyone to follow this suggestion instead of sitting for hours without inquiring. If you were seated in a restaurant, had given your order for food, and none was ever served to you, how long would you continue to sit there?

When we finally got into an exam room, the doctor put on gloves and checked Al's throat because of his frequent coughing and nasal drainage. He tossed the used tongue depressor toward the trashcan, but it missed and fell on the floor. The doctor picked it up in his gloved hand and tossed it a second time, this time making the shot. Then he continued to examine Al with the gloved hand that had touched the floor. Red flag!

My insides lurched. Should I stop him? Should I say something? How far should I ride this broom? My heart was screaming, *PLEASE! He's already had enough infections!*

The Home Health nurse had asked if she could accompany us to the doctor's appointment in order to get a better handle on things. Wonderful! It was on her own time. I was ecstatic. When it was time to see the doctor, he didn't want us to put Al on the table because "he may fall."

I stated, "I would NEVER let him fall!"

I was adamant to follow this thing through, and so the nurse and I hoisted Al onto the exam table. When the nurse unpacked the wound, which now was large enough to hold two 4x4 gauze pads, the doctor was appalled. A long Q-tip could easily be inserted into the tunnels leading out from the hole in the flesh at least three inches–and three fingers wide! Guilt overwhelmed me for once again not being able to prevent this horrible thing from escalating and causing Al all this pain and suffering.

As he began to touch the area with the gloved hand that had picked up the used tongue depressor from the floor, I prayed, *Lord, please don't allow infection to take hold. Help me, Lord, not to ever again keep quiet about important things. I must learn to speak up.*

The doctor started a rehearsed monologue about what causes the sores.

I interrupted with, "I *know* what causes the sores."

He continued, "This area is Stage Two, this is Stage Three."

I interrupted again. "Doctor, I know all of that. What I want to know is, WHAT ARE WE GOING TO DO ABOUT IT?"

It was obvious he did not know what to do and couldn't believe his eyes. I believe he made up a treatment plan on the spot. You be the judge.

He ordered boiling out the wound with *peroxide*, then packing it with peroxide-soaked gauze. Again my insides rebelled. I am not a nurse or doctor and have not had any medical training, but I just get this foreboding; a red flag goes up. I may not even have a basis for the reluctance, but I just know in my "knower." I suggest that if you have that feeling, follow it. I believe it's from God.

But the nurse nodded and agreed to do as he said. Now it was two against one. Should I have challenged his instructions? I didn't. The treatment plan was followed until we went back to the surgeon ten days later. I could hardly bring myself to do the regimen. Why didn't I call the surgeon? He was out of town.

At our next appointment, the surgeon inquired what we were doing at the GP's instruction. I told him and he shook his head. A look of disbelief and disappointment clouded his face when he saw the deteriorated condition of the wound. He explained that peroxide should never be in direct contact with the tissue for an extended period of time.

What did I tell you? I knew intuitively that couldn't be right. But we have to do what the doctor says, right?

We changed doctors, but the change appeared to be not a satisfactory one. So we changed again.

Lord, please lead us to a compassionate person who will care for Al with expertise and professional knowledge, someone we can trust. Thank You for Your tender care for Your children.

CHAPTER TWENTY-SIX

"YAWN"

"**Y**es, come on, we'll work you in" means waiting almost two hours to see the doctor.

When the new specialist finally came in he asked the reason for Al's last hospitalization. Was he having chest pains? Did he have shortness of breath? Were there any signs of heart problems? All negative. I explained that I had taken him to the GP because of a persistent productive cough, poor appetite, and a low-grade fever. The doctor said Al was dehydrated and needed to go to the hospital right away.

The cardiologist explained what he thought probably happened according to the records I took with us, showing that Al had had a myocardial infarction some time earlier. I am aware that doctors almost always consult, but I had requested that the GP not have contact with the cardiologist before our visit because I wanted to get a fresh opinion, unbiased and not influenced by a doctor seen previously. It was more for me than it was for Al. I wanted to see if we could make a few changes in his medication to improve Al's quality of life.

Somewhere during the consultation, suspicion formed. I picked up on certain phrases and terminology that had been used by the GP, who had told me it was a waste of time to see a cardiologist. "I can do for him right here–you don't need to waste the time and money for a specialist."

I allowed the cardiologist to finish then asked, "Has the GP called here and talked to you?"

"I have not talked to him personally, but, yes, he called and talked to my staff."

I queried, "No follow-up visit, no further testing, no medication changes?"

"Oh, well, I guess you could reduce the diuretic and reduce the potassium; the heart is only working at 15 – 20 percent. He has about two years to live," the doctor said nonchalantly.

"But nothing can be done to let the blood pressure come back up to normal so he won't feel so tired and want to sleep all the time? 92/56 is not a good BP. Even I know that!" I pleaded.

"No, keep everything else the same."

My insides knotted up. I was absolutely seething, but I kept my cool and thanked him for his time. As we left his office, I agonized internally over the GP who wasn't there. *Why did you betray my trust? Why did you go behind my back? Why did you sabotage this visit when I told you I didn't want corroboration?*

I stomped down the hall, pushing Al in his wheelchair, punched the DOWN button on the elevator, stormed through the automatic doors, and wheeled out to the parking garage where I had left the van. I had parked in a handicap space with blue slanted lines next to it for space to let down the ramp. Alas, when I arrived back at the van, someone had parked inside the blue lines. *Grrr!*

Not being able to open the side door, I had to take Al back to the entrance of the building to wait alone until I could bring the van around. As I got to the front door, a sweet lady waiting for her ride offered to stay with Al until I returned. She was so happy to do a good deed. Thank God that even in our dark circumstances He provided a help for me so I wouldn't worry over leaving Al. I went back to the van and drove to the front entrance to retrieve Al. I was just about spent.

The gaping hole in my heart needed to be filled. I needed comfort. *Lord, why did they let me down?*

We drove home where I wrote a one-paragraph letter to the GP stating that we would not be back because he had violated my trust. A week later I received a letter from him denying that he or his staff had any contact with the cardiologist. What am I to believe? Either way, I couldn't feel confident after that.

CHAPTER TWENTY-SEVEN

SURVIVAL MODE

Several more months went by. Springtime arrived. Al's blood pressure was 78/56, his oxygen level was 90 and below, and his heart rate was always above 120. He had diarrhea for several days, and the wound on his sacrum showed no signs of healing. Because his head had to be elevated to help him breathe, which in turn placed additional pressure on the pelvic area, this began causing even more sores. We discontinued the wound vac because the tape that had to be used caused an allergic reaction. His nutrition level suffered because of his poor appetite even though we used protein powder, shakes, vitamins, and a number of things to boost his dietary intake. He simply was not doing well.

We had spent eight days in the hospital four weeks before. Once during her daily visit the Home Health nurse strongly recommended we go to the emergency room. As soon as she finished her treatment and left, we dressed and prepared to go back to the hospital.

Settling into a room in the hospital, the standard requirement again was the airflow mattress, and this time, because of the severe diarrhea, we had to use very expensive special pads that allowed the air to come through but still provided moisture-proof protection.

Built-up fluid in Al's lungs masked the results of chest

X-rays. Kidney function that was never affected before began to wane. A urologist evaluated Al, saw the extensive amount of fluid, considered dialysis, and ordered a diuretic. But thankfully he was conservative in his treatment plan because of Al's reduced heart function. And I was praying. The next day when the urologist came in, after studying Al's latest blood work and observing his increased urine output, he noticed that the edema in Al's feet and legs had diminished considerably. Praise God! I was relieved. The doctor decided to continue the same conservative treatment and see if the desired results continued.

New antibiotics that supposedly would not cause a reaction were started in order to stop the diarrhea. Al broke out with a horrible rash. The antibiotic medication had to be discontinued immediately. This time a medicated powder was used for the rash and improvement was almost immediate.

For almost a year, we had been using a powdered thickener in all the liquid Al consumed to prevent him from aspirating. At the hospital, a jelled thickener came in individual packets on his meal trays. Subsequently, I observed that his diarrhea seemed to get worse. His stool actually resembled the gel we were putting into his body.

The director of nursing came to our room on a routine visit and checked to see if we needed anything. When I inquired about changing the thickener to the kind we used at home, she agreed to locate some. When the new thickener was discontinued, his stool changed, but it took awhile because we had used it for several days before I made the connection. I was thankful for her cooperation in obtaining the powdered form.

I phoned the manufacturer's number on the packet to ask if the ingredients could possibly cause diarrhea. Without hesitation, their representative said it was highly possible because it was almost pure fiber and some users had reported that it did cause diarrhea. It seemed unusual to me that no information or warning in this regard was on the packet. *Thank You, Lord, that You helped me to solve this problem.* Powder worked well; gel caused problems.

My heart remained so heavy. I knew that if one is unable to eat or drink over an extended period of time, he cannot survive. I tried so hard. Finding something Al would eat was a constant challenge. I ordered applesauce, pudding, gelatin, fruit, scrambled eggs, grits, oatmeal, dry cereal and banana, ice cream and sherbet. About the fifth day after being admitted, he took a couple of bites of several things and I was ecstatic. I bragged on him and told him how happy he made me by eating something.

Within a few minutes he vomited everything. My hopes sank. Everything had to be changed so I pressed the call button for help, but no one came.

The clean laundry cart was parked just outside our room door so I helped myself to the linen, towels, washcloths, sheets, and gown so I could bathe Al, change his gown, and change his bed. Just as I finished cleaning everything, someone came and offered help, but the job was already done. He vomited again. I called for help again, but no one came. So I took care of the problem myself. Were they learning that if they waited awhile, the job would be finished? *Lord, You know that I am certainly capable of doing this. We have had plenty of experience at home. Forgive me for judging when I don't know all the facts. Help me to understand and not judge.*

Medication for diarrhea didn't help. Medication for his stomach didn't help. His breathing was labored. His blood pressure was very low. But optimism was my motto. Since he had not been up in his wheelchair, which was his routine at home, maybe it would help him to sit up awhile. I suggested they send someone to help me get him up. I soon realized he was actually too ill to sit up. The doctors, while they endeavored to be positive, realized Al's numbers were not very good. Al was losing ground.

Our wound care nurse in the hospital was so skilled and particularly careful with Al. She was a lovely, petite young lady with long, dark hair pulled back revealing her flawless complexion and dazzling smile. She was always cheerful, but her serious side emerged when she started her procedure. Her job was to achieve results. She was organized, knowledgeable, and very adept.

For almost a year Al had been through so much pain in daily treatment of the decubitus, both with Home Health and in the hospital. Our wound care nurse was determined that we would conquer this persistent sore. Her method of cleansing the wound, packing, and dressing it was so precise. As I watched the almost artistic execution of her job I was impressed. She came each day at the same time, and as I held Al in position with a draw sheet, she worked and explained each step she was doing and why. When she finished I felt confident that it was done correctly. *Lord, please bless her abundantly for her compassion and care. Thank You for sending us someone so competent.*

Her efforts paid off. Within a few days we began to notice improvement. It wasn't our imagination. It was reality. Her smiles broadened and accompanied her expression of relief and success.

Two days following the decubitus victory, the three doctors—the general practitioner, the cardiologist, and the urologist—all bearing negative reports came one by one throughout the day. Individually, they tried to encourage me to consider placing Al in a nursing home, putting in a feeding tube, and calling in hospice and various other possibilities for his continued care. There was simply nothing else they could do. He was not eating, his urine output with medication was acceptable but not normal, and his vitals were slipping rapidly.

I listened, my brain shrouded in a fog, my heart breaking,

my spirits dashed. *How can I process this news without falling apart? Lord, PLEASE help me! Help me think and make the right decision for Al. I know in my mind that the right decision for me is to take him home and care for him as usual. Is that what is right for Al? Only I can do this!*

When they finished, my response was negative. Through tears I rejected any suggestion that meant someone else would care for Al.

I told them, "He will go home when you release him, and I will care for him and love him and do everything he needs."

Their questions continued: "Who will help you? Do you have children? Do you have Home Health?" *Why all these questions?*

I replied, "It is a full-time job, I will admit, but that honor and privilege is mine and mine alone." *Please see my heart in this. Can you hear my insides screaming? This is my beloved! In sickness and in health!*

The primary care doctor had seated himself. He spoke gently and patiently, explaining what he expected would happen with Al's condition in the very near future. I had to steel myself against what seemed to be the inevitable, all the time resisting and rejecting what he was saying. *No! This can't be happening! You have to fix him! He* will *pull out of this!* When he saw he was getting nowhere, he shook his head, stood up, hugged me, and told me to call him if I needed anything. I promised I would.

Did I detect tears in his eyes? Thank You, Lord, for the compassion I feel from this medical professional. Is what I'm feeling called denial? Then I have it, big-time!

The director of nursing followed the doctor's visit and offered her help as well. She tried to answer any questions that came up regarding Al's care. I knew it would not be easy.

Al was still not taking any nourishment. He actually was not eating or drinking except maybe a sip at a time. As soon as he swallowed, I could hear the liquid gurgling through his stomach and intestines. Within a short time, it had gone through his body. My insides wept. But I would continue to smile and hug him and talk about going home soon. *O Lord! Will we really get to go home? Please, God.* He still had ongoing diarrhea, congestive heart failure, MRSA, and all the other things. I sat beside his bed, whispering my love, touching him, caressing his face, kissing him tenderly, and reassuring him that I was there.

When his breathing became rhythmic, indicating he had finally fallen asleep, I'd tiptoe over to the fifth-floor window of our room and stare out at the city lights. Traffic slowed during the wee hours, but activity never stopped. Life, death, pain, and suffering continued in the darkness with the periodic wail of a siren now and then signaling that someone somewhere needed help. On our very floor, people were hurting and probably wondering when the night would ever end. *Lord, at times You seem so far away. Are You aware of our aloneness? Can You read all this grief in what's left of life?*

God came through with comfort. "Can a woman forget her nursing child? . . . I will never forget you. Behold, I have graven you upon the palms of My hands" (Isaiah 49:15a, 16a).

Yes, the nights were so long, but God was there with us. Isaiah 43:2, 4, and 5a reassured me saying, "When you pass through the waters, I will be with you and when through the rivers, they shall not overwhelm you; when you go through the fire you shall not be scorched; or through the flames you shall not be burned . . . because you are precious in my eyes you are honored and I love you . . . fear not therefore for I am with you."

Sunday finally dawned. The world seemed to awaken, but for Al daylight was immaterial. We again tried to get him to eat and kept any bathing or disturbance to a minimum. Time for wound care came and went. I stepped to the nurses' station three doors down the hall to inquire a number of times who would be taking care of Al's wound that day. The regular wound care specialist was off for the weekend, and no one knew who was to take her place.

Five hours later, an RN and her assistant gowned up and came in. The RN was attractive, well-groomed with perfectly coiffed hair, sporting an abundance of mascara, artistically placed lip liner, and a crisp white uniform. She didn't speak to me but seemed at that moment to be fully in charge. She assessed the wound care materials, took the gown off, and went for supplies. Returning, she donned another gown and gloves, put down the supplies, and realized she had forgotten something. Gown off, get forgotten supplies, gown on for the third time, each time a fresh gown. She asked the assistant to please get a still missing item in her inventory.

At this point, I looked beyond her physical appearance and mentally questioned her ability to do this job. Her movements became erratic, and her scattered conversation with the assistant was jumbled and disconnected. She seemed haphazard and disorganized to say the least. I thought maybe she was having a bad day. I had seen this nurse working at the nurses' station, but she had never been assigned to our hall. I finally placed it—yes, she reminded me of a Barbie doll.

Meanwhile, I had prepared Al to be in position for the procedure. My heart was so heavy after the edict from all the doctors. *How can I face this? What is going to happen? God, I need You more than ever now. Please help me! Yes, I remember Your Word from Isaiah 40:29-31. "They that wait upon the Lord shall renew their strength; they shall mount up with wings as eagles, they shall run and not be weary, they shall walk and not faint." Teach me, Lord, to wait.*

"Barbie" finally spoke only a few words in greeting after she organized her supplies. Putting on gloves, I was ready with the draw sheet holding Al on his side. She saw that Al's bottom was still red from the previous bout of diarrhea. She told the assistant to get a certain tube of cream. I immediately interrupted and told her Al was allergic to that particular cream, and we were now using a medicated powder.

"Oh, we use this on everybody. Nobody is ever allergic to this. It will help a lot," she insisted. I began to cry and begged her to please not use it on Al.

When her assistant returned with the offending cream, Barbie grabbed the tube and squeezed out about a quarter of a cup into her gloved hand and spread it all over his bottom. I looked at the ceiling and stifled my sobs. She peered at me, perhaps assessing my emotions, and quipped, "I've been doing wound care a long time, and I know what I'm doing! What is *wrong* with you?"

Why could I not tell her what was wrong with me? Why did I allow her to verbally abuse me? Why did I lie down emotionally and let her tromp on me? Why couldn't I stand up to her in Al's defense? Had I simply run out of steam?

Tears dripped off my chin as I held the draw sheet. She grabbed a dry washcloth and wiped the cream off her gloved hand. Then she reached for the gauze to pack the wound with the same gloves that she had just used on Al's bottom.

I gasped. "Please, please! Change your gloves!" I begged between sobs. I reached across Al to the tray with my gloved hand and handed her fresh gloves from the box.

"Oh, all right," she grumbled. She changed one glove. Then, holding the gauze over the trashcan, she poured saline on the entire roll. I gasped again. In hindsight, I realize it was at this point I should have dismissed her. Why didn't I have the courage?

"No, please," I pleaded. "The wound care nurse has packed it dry and it has improved beautifully. I would like for us to continue what is working."

She visibly bristled then snarled at me that the instructions were in the book and she was following instructions. She had her assistant go get the chart to prove her point. By that time, I was sobbing unashamedly, still holding Al in place and still hoping she would listen to me.

Continuing to do the wound care she supposedly knew so well, she forgot the medicine to be applied around and on the wound, failed to apply the sterile skin prep to protect Al from the tape, wadded up about five or six squares of gauze and plopped them onto the sore, and stuck a piece of tape across it. By that time I was in a panic. *Let it go. When she leaves, you can fix it yourself.* I tried to get control of myself.

I certainly wasn't prepared for her next remark. She glared at me once again over her glasses and said, "Where is your family? Why isn't someone here to help you?"

Still crying, I whispered, "I have no family; are you going to penalize me for that?"

"Well, you need someone here with you," she barked. The assistant had stepped outside the door and saw that two visitors were waiting to see me. The two nurses encouraged me to go on and see the visitors. Since my mission of holding Al in place was done, I pulled off my gloves, dried my tears, kissed Al, and told him I would be right back. I burst into tears of relief when I saw two dear friends, thankful I had someone to hug me and comfort me, someone who wouldn't beat me up. We walked down the hall and found a seating area where we could talk. What a blessing they had come! God orchestrated the timing on that one.

Shortly after we were seated, Barbie came down the hall, interrupted without apology, and announced that she had finished and Al was resting. "His hair smelled funny so I washed his hair and cleaned his face. Oh, and I also straightened the room."

I was so embarrassed, but I simply thanked her and she left. I couldn't think. What did she mean, his hair smelled funny? I washed his hair regularly with our special brought-from-home shampoo. What did she use to wash it? How did she wash it? Did she comb it when she finished? Where did she find his comb? Why did she have to say that in front of my guests? Sensing my anxiety to get back to Al, my friends left shortly afterward.

When I entered the room, there Al lay with his wet hair standing up, a towel on his pillow, and a bottle of body wash open on the tray. Yes, it hurt my pride for her to say his hair smelled funny, because I was very conscientious about taking care of Al, keeping him well-groomed and dressing him carefully. *Lord, does my pride need to be worked on? It's going to take a lot of correction and repentance to bring me out of this. Please help me now!*

I washed his hair again, dried it, and combed it in his normal style. I turned him just a little and removed the wad of gauze from under the bandage, took out the wet gauze, but that was as far as I could go. I couldn't fix the rest of it.

On Monday the regular wound care nurse came in at her appointed time. When she greeted us cheerfully, I blurted out that she could never leave again. She smiled and asked why, but I told her it would be better left unsaid. "You see, I don't want to get anybody in trouble." *Lord, why am I fearful? Something needs to be done.* This was an opportunity to explain what happened, because all the evidence was directly in front of us. When the health of a patient is jeopardized someone is responsible.

I had heard horror stories of family members "ratting out" nurses who didn't perform their duties properly, and the nurses later took their revenge upon the family members' hospitalized loved one. I sure didn't want Al to be their victim, so I was hesitant to tattle.

As I held Al with the draw sheet, the wound care nurse took one look at the poorly applied bandage, removed it, and groaned. "What happened to our victory of improvement?" I didn't have to tell her; she could see that actual damage had been done. She finished Al's wound care and left the room to find the person who had taken care of him over the weekend.

Soon the director of nursing appeared in our room, sat

down, and looked as if she planned to stay awhile. Taking notes, she began to ask numerous questions I hesitated to answer. She promised me it was necessary and I would not get anyone in trouble. She would take it from there, and yes, there would be consequences.

Word traveled fast. When the nurses came in they individually asked me if they were doing all right. *Is there anything I can get for you? Am I doing anything wrong or neglecting to do something you want me to do?* Isn't it strange? I had repeatedly asked one of them to please pull the curtain and close the door each time she finished. But she never did, so I had to get up and do it myself. After news of the others' offenses leaked, I never had to ask her to pull the curtain or close the door again.

The good news came one afternoon when the doctor said we could go home. Twelve days was a long time, but it had finally come to a close. Al was still in grave condition, but he was ready for me to dress him in his bright raspberry shirt, khaki slacks, and take him home. I promised him some homemade potato soup and anything else he could think of that he wanted to eat.

I wheeled Al out to the van and into the beautiful sunshine. Freedom! What a beautiful drive home. Home sounded so wonderful. He made the trip just fine and wanted to stay up awhile after we arrived home.

Friends were waiting on our porch to welcome us and help us carry things in. How thoughtful! It was inviting just to think about getting into our own bed that night. Our dear neighbor called early in the evening to ask if I needed help transferring Al. He knew Al's fluid buildup was added weight and doing this by myself would be difficult. He came, and even with our expert coordination we executed the first transfer in a rather clumsy manner. But with only one more rehearsal, we had it down to a science. How wonderful to have two extra arms for assistance!

We followed this routine each night starting at 10 p.m. It took almost forty-five minutes to get Al comfortable and settled. What a faithful neighbor to lend his assistance seven days a week!

Lastly, we would have a prayer together. All of them were precious and usually contained a commitment to a good night of rest. But one phrase stood out to me that I will remember always. Our friend prayed, ". . . and, Lord, love Al through the night, in Jesus' name. Amen."

Following the "amen," Al would fall asleep almost immediately.

CHAPTER TWENTY-EIGHT

DREAMS SPEAK VOLUMES

Several nights later I had a disturbing dream. In the dream, I was expecting company so naturally I needed to clean and straighten the house. I opened the door to one room in the "house" and it was full—filled to the doorway with boxes, packages, mounds of "stuff," with nothing labeled and no indication as to the contents of these containers. Dust and debris were everywhere. I closed the door and turned to assess the rest of the house; it was messy. The broom in my hand was ineffective as I tried to bring order to the chaos.

When I awoke, I knew God was speaking to me. My life had become filled with rubbish, hurts, defenses, and pushed-back experiences shut away in almost impenetrable containers, some even conveniently forgotten, not even labeled to identify what they were about; nevertheless they were stored rather than released, cleansed, and forgiven.

Prior to this dream I asked God to confirm to me His promises regarding Al's condition, which seemed to be at a standstill. Various and sundry treatments seemed to have no effect on the physical wounds that had escalated rather than reversed. My frustration was aimed at the lack of knowledge of treatments–seemingly more trial and error than actual tried-and-true treatment to bring healing. Put a man on the moon, but watch this sore become a chasm!

As I turned to the Word of God one day, I read Jeremiah 30:17: "I will restore health to you and I will heal your wounds." So I held onto that promise for Al.

But this morning, I was asking God to speak to me, comfort me, help me to let go–and the dream came to my mind. In speaking with a dear friend whose spiritual discernment I trust, she said, "It's *you* who need healing and restoration. *Your* wounds need to be healed." With this realization, I asked God to walk with me as I went to "open the door" to the room containing all the packages representing hurts, anger, wounds, disappointments, shattered dreams . . . All the stuff I had pushed back, packaged up, and shut off, things I had locked away to steel myself from further wounding.

"Lord," I cried, "please heal my wounds, restore emotional health to me . . ."

This will be a process, I know, because He will have to go piece by piece and deal with the individual "sores" I haven't even acknowledged much less addressed. But thank God, He will bring healing, restoration, and freedom as I'm willing to hear His voice and let Him do a work in me . . . "to conform me to the image of His Son."

What happens as we travel the road of care giving is that we meet the challenges to the best of our ability, take care of the immediate problem, ride our brooms, and do whatever we have to do to get the job done, and "stuff" the junk back to take care of later. The result is that many times the "stuff" never gets the attention it needs, so we become bitter, resentful, and unforgiving and build walls so the hurt won't hurt so badly. Most of the time we're not even aware that we have closeted the hurts which eventually grow the roots of bitterness that consume us until it's too late.

My prayer was that as I faced each challenge I would see God's hand working in my life to "conform me." I must let go of each of the "packages" at the moment He targeted it. *O Lord, help me!*

CHAPTER TWENTY-NINE

HOME . . . FOREVER

*H*ow wonderful it felt to be home.

A sip of orange juice, two hours later a swallow of tomato soup or a bite of applesauce. Victories were small but I celebrated each one. I rejoiced because Al had no other means of intake. No feeding tube, no IVs.

Many times during the day, since we came home from the hospital, I carried food and drink, any kind of nourishment I thought Al would like and that his body would tolerate. Home Health nurses came each morning to clean and pack the unhealed wound that developed during a hospital stay exactly one year ago.

Rollercoaster emotions ruled, up one minute, down the next. Congestive heart failure necessitated suctioning his throat when he coughed. Sometimes he resisted and bit the tube. I tried so hard not to hurt him, but it must have been uncomfortable. Fluid was still a problem, but his urine output looked pretty normal even though his intake was so limited. I wondered how long this could continue.

I thought if he could sit up in the wheelchair he would feel better. He always liked getting dressed, so even though it was late in the day I put on his brightest shirt and got him up. He could breathe easier in an upright position, but he was so weak I felt guilty for having encouraged it.

When our neighbor and I put Al to bed each night, weakness in his body caused sleep to overtake him immediately. His breathing was labored but regular.

A longtime friend who as a teenager had attended Al's first church, now retirement age, came on Wednesday from her home in Virginia to say "goodbye." She helped me prepare food, answer the phone, clean the house, and do laundry. What a blessing!

Both during the day and for two nights I lay on the bed beside Al, holding him, talking softly to him, using the suction when necessary. I kept the lamp on and played soft Christian music on the radio–and I prayed. All night as he lay with his eyes closed, his oxygen level hovered at about 90 percent, then 89, then 88, gradually slipping. His heart rate was erratic between 70 and 125. We stopped taking his blood pressure because his arms bruised so easily.

Due to a back problem, our friend chose to sleep on the floor in the living room, but periodically she tiptoed in to check on us. As she sat beside the bed, she crooned encouragement and loving words to Al. Her mother had died several years before from congestive heart failure. She struggled and gasped, panicked because she was unable to take enough oxygen into her lungs. Our friend relived the nightmare yet was thankful that Al was not having the awful pain her mother had suffered. *Thank You, Lord, for Your mercy. Al doesn't seem to be struggling.*

The hours of darkness, both outside and in my heart, stretched on, endless. How long could this continue? Constant prayers flowed from my being. *O God! Thank You for extending Your mercy. Thank You for this servant of Yours who loves You. Thank You that Your will be done. Help me, Jesus!* Hours crawled by.

Sunday morning at 5:25, Al missed a breath. I remembered my mother's final hours. *O God! O God!* I wept uncontrollably. *How can I bear this?*

My love, my sweetheart, my darling! Life itself as well as hope is ever so silently being wrenched from me as I observe the impossible situation happening before me. In the midst of the trauma, wonderful memories began to surface. Walking together across a swinging bridge on our wedding trip (Al refused to call it our honeymoon because, as he said romantically, "We will always be on our honeymoon"), riding the Matterhorn together at Disneyland, taking off together on my first plane ride, squeezing Al's arm so tightly I left finger marks, reliving his carrying me across the threshold to celebrate together moving into our first house we had purchased, walking together to the back door of the church when he finished preaching on Sundays. *O Lord! What if there is to be no more "together"? How can I possibly go on without him?*

His breathing was still regular but labored. His eyes were closed. I remembered hearing somewhere that even if a patient doesn't respond he can still understand and that the sense of hearing is the last to go. I continued to talk to Al; inside I was crying out to God. *Please, Lord! Hold me! Hold Al!*

Our friend was on the other side of the bed. She was exactly who needed to be with us. God provided everything we needed, even though we didn't know what that was.

Denial had prevented my thinking about when and how this moment would actually come, so I never anticipated what it would be like. But God knew and prepared the way with persons and timing and mercy and comfort.

Then, with no additional struggle or unrest, Al quietly coughed twice . . . and never took another breath. The digital clock registered 7:10 a.m., May 22, 2011.

. . . in sickness and in health, till death do us part.

EPILOGUE:
WHAT NOT TO SAY

*M*ichael Card recorded a song that says, "We all use so many different clumsy words, most of the words we often say are not worth being heard." A friend of mine added, "Some of the words we do say shoot straight to the heart; if we're not careful, we can tear someone's life apart." Permit me to embellish on this thought for a moment.

It's human nature I suppose to think we must say something upon encountering each of life's situations. Please trust me. Some things are better left unsaid. I could write a book of the various statements and remarks people made to me when they learned of Al's death.

I myself have probably said something offensive many times, more than the average person, but if you and I can learn a little and spare someone the pain caused by our stupidity, I will deem this epilogue worthwhile.

Listen to yourself. Ask yourself, "How will this sound to my grieving friend? Will it help or hurt?" If you don't trust yourself, just leave it unsaid and give the other person a warm hug.

"I know just how you feel." *No, no! No one ever has the same hurt, sadness, or loss another feels because relationships are all different. You may have felt some of the same feelings, but you don't know* just *how I feel. I knew one lady very well whose husband of fifty years had died. She told me a short time later that the past months without him had been the best time of her life. Yet she said she knew just how I felt. That sounds like a gross exaggeration; nevertheless it's a true story.*

"I understand what you're going through; I lost my ____." Then they go on to describe the loss of a cousin or parent or friend. *How can it be compared at all? Again, relationships are all different, with different levels and intensities.*

"He's in a much better place." *His place was beside me for, lo, these many years. And I miss his being here with me so dreadfully.*

"You wouldn't want him back." *Wrong! Wrong! Why would I not want him back? I miss him!*

"Now that he's gone, you can have a life again." *He was my life! Enough said.*

"God said He would never put more on us than we can bear." *What does that mean? Who knows when the limit is reached?*

Please don't require an explanation for each of these. Just think!

"<u>Now</u> you can come and visit us."

"As soon as possible, get rid of everything that reminds you of him."

"Are you going to stay in the area?"

"A lot of times, when a spouse dies, the one who is left doesn't live much longer."

"If you need anything, just call me."

"Is someone staying with you at night?"

"I'm glad to see you haven't let yourself go."

"You're still young enough to ____."

"You have to eat! You're losing so much weight you're about to blow away!"

"Are you sleeping all right?

"It will take a while, but just stay busy. It will get better."

"He's healed now."

Think on each of these remarks. Can you try to understand how painful this is? As I shared some of these remarks with a dear friend, she declared that the people who made them actually meant well. "They didn't mean to hurt you, I'm sure; they were just trying to help."

How kind of her to say that. I wish I could accept it. I'm trying to give them the benefit of the doubt. Could I suggest what would have blessed me more?

"I'm sorry. I love you."

"I'll watch your lawn. When it needs to be cut, I'll come and do it–no charge. Don't worry about it."

"I'm bringing a casserole this afternoon. It freezes well for later if you don't feel like eating it now."

"Would you like to come for dinner?"

"I'm praying for you."

"I'm in town. Do you need anything? I'll stop by or leave it on your porch."

The less said the better. "Among a multitude of words, transgression is not missing, but he who restrains his lips is prudent" (Proverbs 10:19).

To My Friend in Your Grief
It seems so useless to say,
"Is there anything I can do for you?"
I know what I can do.
If you want company,
I will stay with you.
If you want to be alone,
I will leave my love with you.
If you want to talk,
I will listen;
If you want to listen,
I will talk.
If you want to be quiet,
I will commune with you in silence.

If you want to eat,
I will serve you;
If you refuse to eat,
I will understand.
Yes, my friend, there is something I can do for you.
I can share your hurt
And maybe make it easier to bear.
Most of all,
I will lift your name in prayer,
Seeking your comfort.
I will help you carry your sorrow to the feet of Jesus,
Who has promised "peace that passes understanding."
Dear friend, I love you.
Anonymous

I'm sure the well-meaning people out there will continue to ask painful questions. At the same time, I will continue to hurt. My prayer is that they will become wiser and I will hurt less.

In the movie *Tootsie* Terri Garr's character says, "I'll just have to feel this way until I don't feel this way anymore."

CPSIA information can be obtained at www.ICGtesting.com
Printed in the USA
LVOW05s2148020514

384069LV00002B/3/P